# Energy, Economics, and the Environment

## Case Studies and Teaching Activities
## for Elementary School

D1287544

**Indiana Department of Education**
**Center for School Improvement and Performance**

**Originally published 1994**

**Revised 2006**

# *Acknowledgements - Original Edition*

## Curriculum Designers/Authors

*Harlan Day, Economics Education Consultant*
Indiana Department of Education

*Deborah Christopher, Teacher*
Delaware Community Schools

*Kate Ferguson, Teacher (retired)*
Fort Wayne Community School Corporation

*Pam George, Teacher*
Northwest Allen County Schools

## Corporate Sponsors

Indiana Michigan Power

Indianapolis Power and Light Company

Northern Indiana Public Service Company

PSI Energy

## Curriculum Committee

*Marty Alenduff*
Indiana Department of Education

*David Ballard*
Indiana Department of Education

*Mike Brian*
Indiana Michigan Power

*Sam Carman*
Indiana Department of Natural Resources

## Supporting Agencies

Indiana Department of Commerce

Indiana Department of Education

Indiana Department of Environmental Management

Indiana Department of Natural Resources

Indiana Michigan Power

Indiana NEED Project

Indiana Petroleum Council

Indianapolis Power and Light Company

IUPUI Center for Economic Education

Northern Indiana Public Service Company

PSI Energy

## Special Recognition

Center for School Improvement and Performance, Indiana Department of Education,
for coordinating and supervising the development of the EEE curriculum
(Special thanks to Christy Skinner for preparing the many drafts and final draft).

Rosanne Russell, Division of Publications, Indiana Department of Education,
for preparing the camera ready final draft.

PSI Energy, for preparing the front cover.

Linda Lentz, teacher at Indianapolis Public School #68, and her students,
for field testing activities in the EEE curriculum.

PSI Energy, Indiana Michigan Power, and Northern Indiana Public Service Company,
for printing the EEE Curriculum.

## Commitment to EEE Program

The EEE program will be promoted through workshops, institutes, and conferences
for teachers.  We welcome new EEE members who believe in the philosophy and
goals of the EEE curriculum.  For further information, contact the
Indiana Department of Education (800-527-4930)
or the Indiana Council for Economic Education (765-494-8545).

# *Acknowledgements – 2006 Revision*

Content review of *Energy, Economics, and the Environment (EEE)* was provided by Mike Ellerbrock, Ph.D., Director of the Virginia Tech Center for Economic Education. Dr. Ellerbock was the 2002 recipient of USDA's National Award for Teaching Excellence in Agriculture, Natural Resources, Human and Veterinary Sciences and is a member of the Governor's Commission on Environmental Education in Virginia.

Sincere thanks are due to Indiana Michigan Power for its ongoing financial support over the years for teacher training programs that support the *Energy, Economics, and the Environment* curriculum. Indiana Michigan Power's dedication to economics education is exemplary.

Royerton Elementary School teacher, Debbie Christopher, gave valuable help in revising the energy and forestry units. Her dedication to energy and economic education is much admired and appreciated.

Shelly Surber, Indiana Council for Economic Education, contributed significantly in the final formatting of this revised publication.

Funding for this revision of *Energy, Economics, and the Environment* was provided by the National Council on Economic Education (NCEE). *Energy, Economics, and the Environment* is distributed exclusively by the NCEE.

**National Council on Economic Education**

1140 Avenue of the Americas
New York, NY 10036
Phone: 212.730.7007 or 1.800.338.1192
www.ncee.net
Email: sales@ncee.net

# Correlation of Energy, Economics, and the Environment: Case Studies and Teaching Activities for Elementary School with the National Standards for Economics*

| ↓ Standards/Lessons → | Introductory Essay | 1 | 2 | 3 | 4 |
|---|---|---|---|---|---|
| 1. Scarcity | √ | √ | √ | √ | √ |
| • Goods & Services | √ | √ | √ | | √ |
| • Producers | √ | √ | √ | | √ |
| • Consumers | √ | √ | | | √ |
| • Productive Resources | √ | √ | √ | √ | √ |
| • Opportunity Cost | √ | √ | √ | √ | √ |
| 2. Marginal costs/marginal benefits | √ | √ | √ | √ | |
| 3. Allocation of goods and services | √ | | | | √ |
| 4. Role of incentives | √ | | √ | √ | √ |
| 5. Gain from trade | | | | | |
| 6. Specialization and trade | | | | | |
| 7. Markets-price and quantity determination | | | √ | √ | √ |
| 8. Role of price in market system | | √ | √ | √ | √ |
| 9. Role of competition | | | | | |
| 10. Role of economic institutions (especially property rights) | √ | | √ | √ | |
| 11. Role of money | | | | | |
| 12. Role of interest rates | | | | | |
| 13. Role of resources in determining income | | | | | |
| 14. Profit and the entrepreneur | | | √ | | √ |
| 15. Growth | √ | | | | √ |
| 16. Role of government | √ | | √ | √ | √ |
| 17. Using cost/benefit analysis to evaluate government programs | √ | | √ | √ | √ |
| 18. Macroeconomy- income/employment, prices | | | | | |
| 19. Unemployment and inflation | | | | | |
| 20. Monetary and fiscal policy | | | | | |

*Voluntary National Content Standards, copyright © 1997 National Council on Economic Education

# Table of Contents

# Rationale

One of the great challenges facing educators is to teach students how to be responsible stewards of the natural resources entrusted to them. This is especially true today since our growing worldwide population inevitably exerts greater strains on our environment and on our fiscal and natural resources. As individuals and as a society, we must be prepared to deal with the problems that will challenge us in the decades ahead. The purpose of the *Energy, Economics, and the Environment* (EEE) curriculum is to provide students with the necessary knowledge and skills to help solve these problems.

The curriculum focuses on three important subjects: energy, economics, and the environment. One of the key assumptions of this booklet is the interrelatedness of these three areas of study. It is virtually impossible to study one of these subjects without encountering the others. Indeed, the failure to consider the interdependence of environmental, energy, and economics issues will result in flawed policy decisions that will diminish the potential for maintaining a strong economic system, a healthy environment, and a sustainable energy resource base.

In order to deal with these complex issues, students must be trained in three important areas. First, they must be taught basic knowledge and concepts about energy, the environment, and economics as well as the fundamental interrelationships of all three. Second, they must learn effective decision-making skills. Third, they must be involved in meaningful, motivating learning activities. As a result of participating in the EEE program, students will understand the trade-offs that are involved in ensuring a quality environment, the wise use of energy resources, and a vibrant economy. Thus, our students will be better equipped to meet the environmental and energy challenges of the future.

# Overview

Nearly every day in the news there are stories dealing with the economic implications of energy and environmental issues. How can students make sense of these complicated issues? What do they need to know in order to make wise decisions as consumers, producers, and voting citizens?

## Purpose of the Energy, Economics, and Environment Curriculum

One purpose of this curriculum is to provide a conceptual framework for analyzing energy and environmental issues, especially in regards to economics. Teachers will notice that Part 1 of the Introduction explains the basic economic concepts that provide the conceptual framework for making wise decisions. Part 2 of the Introduction explains how to use two decision-making models to analyze energy and environmental issues.

A second purpose of this curriculum is to provide teachers with a set of four motivating interdisciplinary teaching units. Unit 1 focuses on basic economic concepts that will help students analyze energy and environmental issues. The excellent, though somewhat dated, video series, Econ and Me, can be used to help teach these economic concepts. The Unit 1 teaching activities are adapted from the *Play Dough Economics* curriculum published by the Indiana Department of Education and distributed by the National Council on Economic Education.

Units 2-4 focus on a particular energy and/or environmental theme. Teachers are provided with factual information about the unit theme and with a set of interdisciplinary teaching activities. The final teaching activity in each unit is a simple case study in which students use a decision-making model to analyze an energy or environmental problem.

The classroom teaching activities require students to apply skills across several areas of the curriculum and also encourage students to make extensive use of resources in their communities. Each unit contains special sections entitled, Let's Talk It Over, Further Explorations, and EEE Actions — You Can Make a Difference!

## A Starting Point for Analysis

The issues covered in teaching Units 2-4 deal with forest, water, and energy resources. These are very complex topics, with new information constantly becoming available. Teachers should therefore view this curriculum as a *starting point for further study*. As you read articles or gather new information about these topics, keep them with the curriculum. This will keep your *Energy, Economics, and the Environment* curriculum up-to-date.

# EEE Curriculum Organization

## Introduction

**Part 1:** **A Framework for Analysis**
- Fundamental Ideas and Relationships
- Three Important Economic Considerations

**Part 2:** **Decision-Making Models: Tools for Analysis**

## Teaching Units

**Unit 1:** **Focuses on basic economic concepts. It uses two popular curriculum materials:**
- Econ and Me
- Play Dough Economics

**Units 2-4:** **Contain these elements:**

**1. Basic Information**
- Overview of the Unit
- Basic Facts About the Issue

**2. Classroom Teaching Activities**
- Teaching Instruction/Key Concepts to Emphasize
- Specific Teaching Activities
- Further Explorations
- Let's Talk It Over
- EEE Actions — You Can Make a Difference!
- Case Study
- Answers to Selected Teaching Activities

# Introduction

## Part 1: A Framework for Analysis

This section provides a general economic framework for analyzing environmental and energy issues. Without such a framework, any analysis of these critical issues will be deficient. Students (future policy makers) must understand the basic economic concepts that relate to these issues in order to make wise environmental and energy policy decisions.

## Fundamental Ideas and Relationships

### The Necessity of Production

In every society, people require **goods** and **services** that will enable them to survive and prosper. *A fundamental principle of economics is that these goods and services must be produced*. Without production of some sort, survival would be virtually impossible.

Fortunately, every society is endowed with resources which can be used to produce goods and services. These resources, called **productive resources (factors of production),** can be classified into three groups: natural resources (land), labor (human) resources, and capital resources. **Natural resources**, both renewable and nonrenewable, come from nature. Examples include coal, water, trees, air, and the land itself. **Labor resources (human resources)** refer to the mental and physical work effort expended in production and to the entrepreneurial skills needed to guide production. **Capital resources** are physical goods used to produce other goods and services such as buildings, tools, equipment, and machinery. Figure 1 illustrates how productive resources are combined to produce goods and services.

The problem for individuals and society is that the desire for most goods and services is **unlimited**, whereas productive resources are **limited**. This tension between unlimited wants and the limited productive resources available for satisfying these wants is what economists refer to as **scarcity**. *Every society, rich or poor, confronts the basic economic problem of scarcity*. [1]

---

1. Note that a distinction exists between the economic notion of scarcity versus the physical concept. For example, economists would say that 4-leaf clovers are *not* scarce, even though there are few of them, if consumers do not desire them.

Figure 1

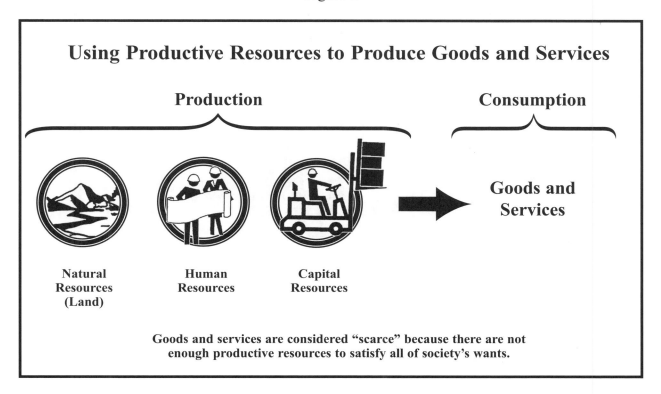

**Using Productive Resources to Produce Goods and Services**

Production      Consumption

Natural
Resources
(Land)  Human
Resources  Capital
Resources

Goods and
Services

Goods and services are considered "scarce" because there are not
enough productive resources to satisfy all of society's wants.

## Production and Energy

So where does energy fit into our discussion? First, *energy is something that consumers desire.*
All of us consume energy in one way or another - to heat our homes, cook our food, or power
our cars.

Second, *energy is necessary for production.* Without some form of energy, the production of
goods and services would virtually cease. Thus, energy is an integral component of both the
production and consumption side of the diagram (Figure 2).

Third, *most forms of energy, like productive resources, are scarce.* With the exception of energy
from the sun, energy resources are not free goods, available in unlimited quantities at a zero
price. Quite the contrary, energy sources are costly to harness, develop, and use. Because
energy is scarce, its value is reflected in our market system by prices. *The price of an energy
resource gives an indication of how scarce the resource is relative to other resources.*

Sometimes an energy shortage may occur, as in the 1970s, when there were long gas lines. A
shortage is caused when a producer or government agency fixes the price of a good or service
below its natural market level. Even when there is no energy shortage, energy is still a scarce
resource. One must still pay to obtain it.

Figure 2

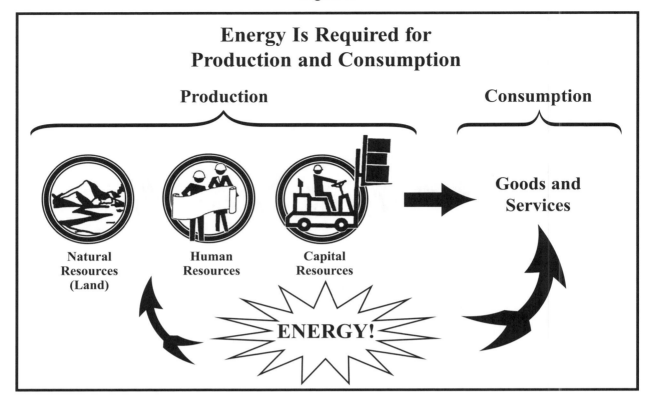

**Energy Is Required for
Production and Consumption**

Production        Consumption

Natural Resources (Land)    Human Resources    Capital Resources

Goods and Services

ENERGY!

## Production and the Environment

Now we can examine how the environment affects our simple model of production and energy use. *All production and consumption must take place within the context of the environment.* As such, the environment affects and is affected by production and consumption. This is evident when examining three basic services provided by the environment.

## Services Provided by the Environment

First, the environment provides us with the **natural resources**, including energy resources, needed to produce goods and services. As we learned above, natural resources are one of the basic productive resources.

Second, the environment is a natural **"waste sink"** for the inevitable by-products/wastes of both production and consumption. In earlier times, organic wastes were more common and were more easily degraded by the environment. However, in modern times many wastes are not easily degraded and are present in larger quantities, resulting in more serious pollution problems for society.

Third, the environment provides us with many **"ecological services"** such as biodiversity, air and water filtration, soil fertility, carbon sequestration, sustainable populations of wildlife, rodent and disease control, scientific knowledge, medical research, pharmacological applications, and natural amenities, such as beautiful wilderness areas, scenic forests, and bodies of water for swimming, boating, and fishing.

Figure 3 expands our production diagram, illustrating the services provided by the environment.

Figure 3

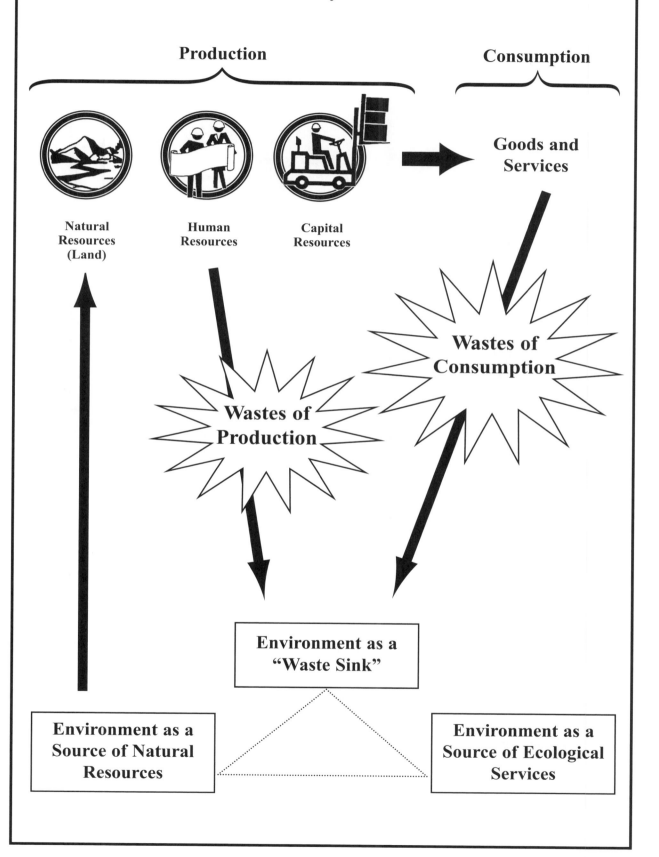

**Services Provided by the Environment**

Production

Consumption

Natural Resources (Land)

Human Resources

Capital Resources

Goods and Services

Wastes of Consumption

Wastes of Production

Environment as a "Waste Sink"

Environment as a Source of Natural Resources

Environment as a Source of Ecological Services

# Summary

The four statements below summarize what we have discussed so far. They provide a starting point for analysis.

---

## A Starting Point for Analysis

1. To survive and prosper, societies must produce goods and services. Every society has productive resources (natural resources, labor resources, and capital resources) that it uses to produce goods and services.

2. Energy is necessary in both production and consumption. Energy sources originate from natural resources. Because most forms of energy are scarce, both producers and consumers must pay to obtain energy.

3. The production and consumption of goods and services generates waste materials, which must be recycled or properly disposed.

4. Using the environment for production, consumption, and waste disposal affects the ecological and amenity services provided by the environment.

---

# Three Important Economic Considerations

There are three critically important economic concepts to consider when analyzing environmental and energy issues: **opportunity cost/trade-offs, spillover costs** (negative externalities), and **marginalism**. They are discussed below.

## 1. Opportunity Cost and Trade-Offs

The basic economic problem of scarcity forces individuals and societies to choose how to use their limited productive resources. For example, money spent purchasing a bicycle cannot be spent on a new television. Tax monies spent on environmental protection and pollution control cannot be spent on national defense. Choices must be made.

Any time a choice is made among alternatives, there are specific alternatives that are *not* chosen. The value of the best alternative *not* chosen is called the **opportunity cost**. *Because productive resources are scarce, there is an opportunity cost to every economic decision.*

When a person or society decides to produce or consume one good instead of another, they are making a **trade-off** - they are trading off less of one thing for more of something else. For example, when a society decides to spend $5 million less on cancer research and instead decides to use the money to purchase land for a national park, the society is trading off better cancer treatment for its citizens for more environmental protection and recreation. It is hoped that the benefits from the park outweigh the potential benefits of the medical research.

The value of what is received when making a trade-off is an estimate of the benefit of the decision. The value of what is given up in making a trade-off is a measure of opportunity cost. The opportunity cost is sometimes measured in dollars, as noted above, where the opportunity cost of using $5 million to help purchase land for a national park is the lost benefits from $5 million *not* invested in cancer research.

Figure 4

# Trade Offs and Opportunity Cost

**Cancer Research**

**National Park**

**$5 Million Dollars**

Society is trading off cancer research for improved environmental protection and recreation. The opportunity cost of choosing a national park is the lost benefits of $5 million dollars spent on cancer research.

One major difficulty in analyzing environmental issues is that it is sometimes difficult to measure the monetary value of opportunity costs. What is the money value of clean air or a clean river? Not surprisingly, individuals differ greatly in this valuation. One person may easily endure moderate amounts of air pollution in a certain area, whereas another person may consider even the smallest amounts of pollution to be intolerable. Despite the difficulty, innovative techniques have been developed by economists to measure opportunity costs to help policy makers when analyzing energy and environmental issues. For example:

- ✔ **Contingent Valuation** – randomized surveys with hypothetical questions asking citizens how much money they would be willing to pay to protect a specific natural resource, or how much they would have to be compensated to accept losing a resource.

- ✔ **Hedonic Pricing** – inferring the value of a specific natural resource based on the changes in value of related goods (e.g., adjacent real estate) that possess some of the same characteristics or provide some of the same services.

- ✔ **Travel Cost Method** – inferring the value of a specific natural resource by extrapolating visitors' actual travel costs to include a hypothetical user fee paid by tourists/sportspersons from various distances to visit the site.

## 2. Spillover Costs

We have learned that the production and consumption of goods and services, including energy, will cause some waste to flow into the environment. This is unavoidable because societies must have goods and services in order to survive and prosper. Also, not all "waste" causes "pollution" because some waste is assimilable by the environment.

However, a major problem arises when the negative effects (costs) of waste flows are imposed on individuals, plants (flora), or animals (fauna) *not* involved in the buying and selling decisions that cause the flows. That is, there are serious problems when the costs of waste flows are imposed on "innocent bystanders" (or ecosystems) who are *external* to the production and consumption decisions that result in the waste flows. Economists refer to these imposed costs as **negative externalities,** or **spillover costs** (Figure 5). In modern times the problem of spillover costs is compounded by the increasing *volume* of waste, as well as by the changing *nature* of waste (less biodegradable, more toxic, etc.).

Air and water pollution is an example of a spillover cost, or negative externality. When a paper mill produces products, it ejects waste materials into the air and water. Individuals who breathe the air near the paper mill or who use the contaminated water bear the brunt of these external costs, even though these individuals may not benefit from the production or consumption of the paper products made in the mill. *An additional problem occurs if no one owns the air or water, and there is therefore no private cost for using these natural resources.* Because the use of the air and water is free, the mill actually has shifted some of the cost of paper production onto other individuals. The result is that too many paper products are produced, and their price is less than it would be if all the costs were taken into account. Also, nearby citizens suffer declining property values and diminished quality of life.

Figure 5

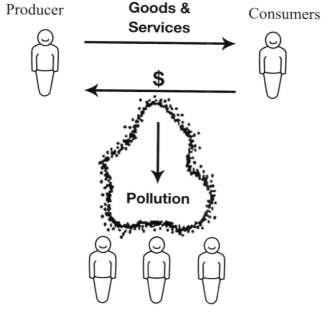

# Pollution Hurts Innocent Bystanders

Producer · **Goods & Services** · Consumers

$

**Pollution**

**Innocent Bystanders**

The producers and consumers both benefit from the production and consumption of goods and services. However, innocent bystanders sometimes receive the negative effects of the pollution created in production. This especially occurs when natural resources used in production, such as air and water, are commonly owned.

## Dealing with Spillovers

What do societies do to correct the effects of negative spillover costs on the environment and on individuals? Some common courses of action are discussed below.

## Rules and Regulations

The most typical way used to reduce spillover costs is through rules and regulations. A government agency (e.g., U.S. EPA, state Department of Natural Resources) may impose regulations which define strict limits on waste discharge or may set certain standards for air pollution or waste disposal. Examples include the mandated emission standards for automobiles or the required use of "coal scrubbers" in plants where coal is the source of energy. Government may even ban a certain type of production all together, as in the case of oil drilling in certain wilderness areas.

Rules and regulations are popular since they seem to provide a simple and direct solution to spillover problems. However, regulations can be costly to implement and enforce. They tend to treat all (major and minor) violators the same, thus raising issues of fairness and efficiency. Regulations also limit individual freedom.

## Taxing Production

Another method used by government (federal or state) is to tax the production activity that produced the spillover. Taxing a product increases its price, thereby reducing the quantity of the product that is produced and consumed. This results in fewer spillover costs, and also raises tax monies that can be used for improving the environment. An example of this method is the excise tax on gasoline, tires, and coal production.

## Subsidies

A third method used by government is subsidies. A subsidy is the opposite of a tax. A government gives money (directly or in the form of tax breaks) to firms to encourage them to reduce spillovers. For example, monies given to a firm may be used to install modern equipment, help clean a river, or revitalize land marred by surface mining. Subsidies may be unpopular since taxpayers may not wish to use public monies to pay for spillovers caused by private firms, even though taxpayers will benefit generally from less pollution in their community.

# Creating Proper Incentives

In recent years, new methods for reducing the harmful effects of negative externalities have been proposed. These methods provide more efficient solutions to spillover problems because they emphasize creating proper incentives for individual action. The goal is to make it more profitable (cost effective) to act in a socially responsible manner.

## Impose Effluent or Emission Taxes

One way to create proper incentives is by imposing effluent or emission taxes. This approach imposes a fee on each unit of pollution discharged into the environment. This tax provides an incentive for firms to devise creative ways to reduce emissions and also provides tax monies for pollution management. Firms could still choose *not* to reduce emissions, but they would have to bear the cost of the decision. The external costs imposed on others would therefore be "internalized." Effluent and emission taxes can be a wise course of action because the tax is on the pollution *discharge*, not the production activity itself. This provides more of an incentive for economic growth and development.

## Define Property Rights

Most economists believe that assigning and enforcing property rights more effectively will create incentives for more responsible social behavior. The logic goes like this: If property is commonly owned, like the air or waterways, it will be overused or abused. In contrast, if property is privately owned, the owner has a strong incentive to maintain or improve the value of the property. For example, a timber company has a financial incentive to harvest forest areas wisely since they are a valuable source of future income. A commonly owned forest is much more likely to be exploited since no individual owner bears the costs.

# Establish Markets for Pollution Rights

Another way to create incentives for responsible care of the environment, consistent with legitimate growth objectives, is to establish markets for pollution rights. For example, a firm that reduces its pollution below the governmental standards could earn "emission reduction credits," which then could be sold to new firms. Under an "offset policy," the new firms would have to buy 1.2 emission credits for each 1.0 units of emissions added by a new plant. Since reductions will be 20 percent greater than additions, the overall air quality would be *improved* every time a new plant entered the area! Similarly, under a "bubble policy," firms cooperate in achieving a stated overall limit on their aggregate emissions.

In studying ways to create proper incentives to improve environmental quality, the main point to emphasize is that in many instances there are creative, practical ways to improve environmental quality instead of imposing rigid regulations that are expensive to enforce and stifle economic growth. It is encouraging to know that strict environmentalists and those in favor of more growth-oriented policies are beginning to recognize that economic development and environmental protection need not inevitably be seen as conflicting goals.

## 3. Marginalism

We have learned that negative externalities are an unavoidable by-product of the production and consumption of goods and services. We have also examined various ways to minimize the harmful effects of these externalities on the environment. A key question remains unanswered, however. How clean should the environment be? It is one thing to agree that action needs to be taken to address a particular environmental problem; it is another to agree to what extent the action needs to be implemented.

## A Problem in Centerville

Suppose that industries in Centerville have so polluted the local river that it is now useless for drinking, swimming, or fishing and is possibly a serious health hazard. While most people would agree that some cleanup is necessary, they may not agree on exactly how *much* cleanup. Fortunately, the concept of **marginalism** helps students analyze these difficult kinds of problems.

In economics, **marginal** simply means "next" or "incremental." This rather simple concept can help us solve the river problem. Suppose all citizens in Centerville agree that some cleanup is necessary. They hire an environmental firm to analyze the situation and report back to the city council. Table I summarizes the firm's findings.

Table I

# Cleaning Up the River

| Degree of Cleanup | Marginal Cost | Total Cost | Marginal Benefit | Total Benefit Cleanup |
|---|---|---|---|---|
| 20 % | $10,000 | $10,000 | $100,000 | $100,000 |
| 40 % | $15,000 | $25,000 | $70,000 | $170,000 |
| 60 % | $25,000 | $50,000 | $50,000 | $220,000 |
| 80 % | $50,000 | $100,000 | $20,000 | $240,000 |
| 100 % | $100,000 | $200,000 | $5,000 | $245,000 |

Common sense tells us that, for a given level of benefits, we should first choose the least costly cleanup method, whatever that may be. The firm's data show that 20 percent of the pollution problem can be solved at a marginal cost of only $10,000. The resulting marginal benefit is a significant $100,000.

The data also show that additional methods could be used to reduce pollution by another 20 percent giving a total degree of cleanup of 40 percent. However, the cost for this next (marginal) 20 percent cleanup has increased to $15,000 resulting in a total cost of $25,000. At the same time, the marginal benefit of this extra cleanup has decreased to $70,000, giving us a total benefit of $170,000.

Notice that as the marginal cost for additional cleanup increases, the marginal benefit of additional cleanup decreases. This makes intuitive sense. Getting the river from 80 percent to a 100 percent pollution-free, pristine condition would be very costly - $ 100,000 - possibly from shutting down some factories altogether and banning any use of power boats. However, the benefit of doing so ($5,000) would not be all that much greater than achieving an 80 percent degree of cleanness.

So how clean *should* the river be? *Economists would say that the citizens of Centerville should continue cleaning up the river as long as the marginal benefits (MB) exceed the marginal costs (MC)*, in this case up to a 60 percent degree of cleanness. Economists call this the point of "optimality," where MB = MC. After that point, the additional costs of cleanup are more than the additional benefits (See Figure 6). The scarce productive resources used for cleanup would be better used for some other purpose.

Students tend to look at the *total* amounts in their analysis. They often recommend a 100 percent degree of cleanup since the total benefit ($245,000) is greater than the total cost ($200,000). However, that would not be the wise choice, as we have demonstrated.

## Automobile Pollution

Another common example that illustrates the concept of marginalism is the case of automobile pollution. One sure way of solving this problem would be banning the use of automobiles altogether. Obviously, the cost to society of doing so would be too great. Instead, our government has mandated the use of pollution control equipment, such as catalytic converters. The logic is that the marginal cost of doing so is less than the marginal benefit to the environment and humans.

To summarize, there are trade-offs and opportunity costs associated with all energy and environmental policy decisions. Thus, it is not wise to implement policies mandating the elimination of *all* negative externalities. Some pollution is inevitable. The key question is *how much*, and that is where marginal analysis is useful.

Figure 6

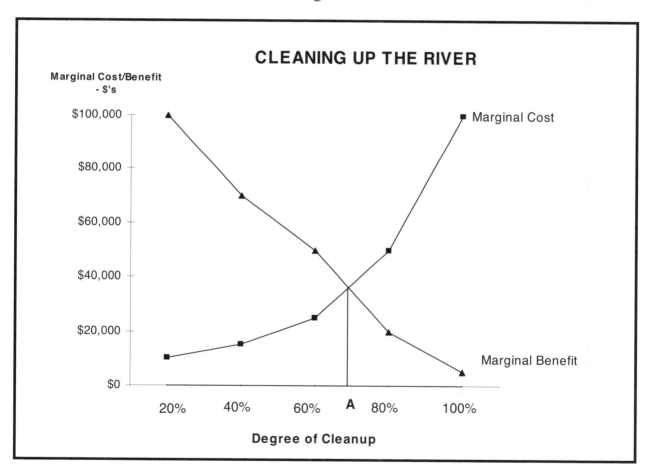

The graph in Figure 6 illustrates the data in Table 1. Notice that the marginal cost increases and the marginal benefit decreases the more the river is cleaned up. After point A, the marginal cost of cleanup exceeds the marginal benefit. Productive resources used to clean the river past point A would best be used elsewhere.

# Summary

So how do we solve the complex environment problems that face us? Below are three points that have emerged from our discussion.

## Ways to Help Improve the Environment

1.  **Be more sensitive to how our production and consumption decisions affect the environment.** Marginal cost/benefit analysis demonstrates that in many cases, steps should be taken to reduce the amount and change the nature of the pollution entering the environment. In production, this means using technologies that create less total waste and less toxic waste. It also means treating industrial wastes to make them more easily assimilated by the environment. In consumption and production, this means reusing and recycling to extend the life of resources and developing safe and effective ways to dispose of waste.

2.  **Develop wise strategies for dealing with spillover costs.** These strategies must attempt to internalize the costs of production so that those who benefit from polluting the environment also bear the costs. These strategies must protect the environment, yet not stifle legitimate economic growth and development.

3.  **Use marginal analysis when deciding how clean the environment should be, recognizing that insisting on a state of zero pollution is usually not the best policy.**

All three courses of action above depend on citizens who are sensitive to environmental issues and who are willing to act in an environmentally responsible manner. In our schools, homes, and churches we must create and foster this important sensitivity.

# Part 2: Decision-Making Models - Tools for Analysis

It is helpful to teach students a systematic way to analyze and solve problems. This gives students a powerful tool to use in their analysis and helps them to organize their thoughts about issues, instead of merely voicing subjective personal opinions. Using a systematic approach to problem-solving also clarifies the trade-offs involved in any solution and reveals the sources of disagreement about various policy alternatives.

## Two Simple Decision-Making Models

There are many problem-solving and decision-making models. The two models used in the EEE curriculum are the **Decision Tree Model** and the **Five-Step Model**. They are both used in the curriculum materials developed by the National Council on Economic Education. Some teachers may want to use more complex models; however, these two are easy to learn and are powerful enough to help solve problems appropriate for elementary students.

The Decision Tree Model and the Five-Step Model are similar. The main difference is that in the Decision Tree Model (see page 19), students list only the two "best" alternatives. In the Five-Step model, students use a Decision Worksheet (see page 20) and a Decision-Making Grid (see page 21) to list multiple alternatives. Students also must list the specific criteria and then evaluate them against the alternatives using a plus/minus marking system. The Decision Tree Model only requires students to list the "good and bad points" about each alternative.

---

### The Decision Tree Model

1. **Define the Problem.** What is the basic problem that needs to be solved?

2. **List the Alternatives.** Identify the two basic alternatives.

3. **Evaluate the Alternatives.** What are the good and bad points of each alternative?

4. **Choose the Best Alternative.** Decide which alternative would be the best in the particular situation.

---

# The Five-Step Decision-Making Model

1.  **Define the Problem.** Analyze the situation. Gather important facts. What is the heart of the problem, the real issue?

2.  **List Alternative Solutions.** Taking into account the reality of scarce productive resources, what are some feasible policy alternatives for solving the problem?

3.  **List Important Criteria.** What are some of the important values and social goals that will influence the decision? Which of these are most important to you or to the community? Who will be helped? Who will be hurt?

4.  **Evaluate the Alternative Solutions.** Use correct economic analysis to evaluate how each alternative "fits" the various criteria.

5.  **Choose the Best Alternative (Make a Decision!)** Which alternative is the most desirable? What are the trade-offs among the different goals/criteria? (How much of one goal must be given up to attain more of another?)

# Decision Tree

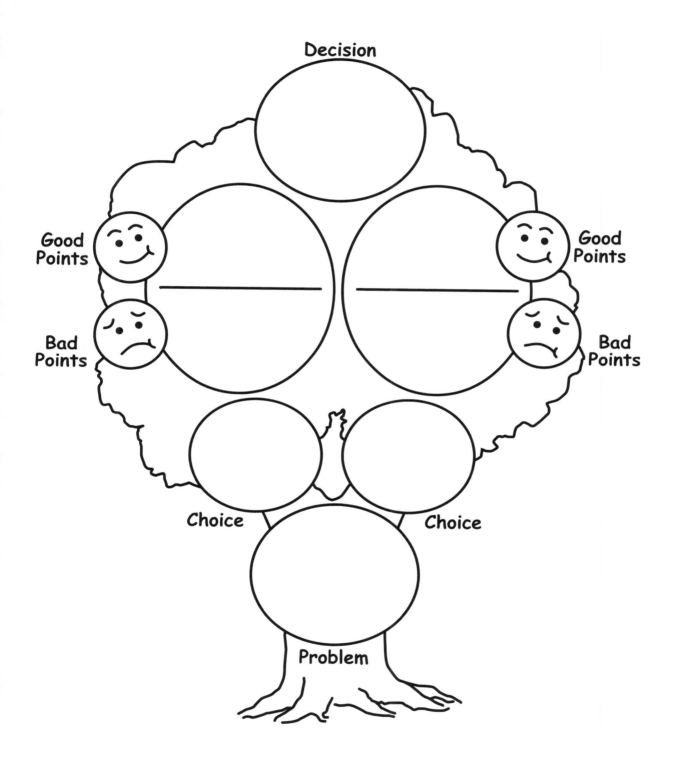

# Decision Worksheet

**Directions:**

1.  Complete this Decision Worksheet and the Decision-Making Grid to help you analyze the problem.

2.  In each cell of the decision grid, your teacher may require you to make a brief comment explaining *why* you made a particular evaluation mark.


STEP 1:  *Define the Problem.*

_____

_____


STEP 2:  *List Alternative Solutions.*

_____

_____

_____

_____


STEP 3:  *List Important Criteria.*

_____

_____

_____

_____


STEP 4:  *Evaluate Alternative Solutions:*
(To do this, fill in the individual cells in the Decision-Making Grid.)

STEP 5:  *Choose the Best Alternative.*

# Decision-Making Grid

| Name | | Class | | |
|------|--|-------|--|--|

| Criteria | | | | |
|----------|--|--|--|--|
| **Alternatives** ↓ | | | | |
| | | | | |
| | | | | |
| | | | | |
| | | | | |
| | | | | |

# Applying the Models – A Simple Case Study

The following case study illustrates how to use the two decision models to solve a problem. This case study is based on the actual legislation found in the 1990 Clean Air Act, which made employer trip reduction programs compulsory in nine metropolitan regions where ozone pollution problems are greatest. These two alternatives are some of those actually recommended by the Environmental Protection Agency (EPA).

## The Case of the Company Carpool

Mr. Samuel Peabody is the president of Best Windows Manufacturing Company, located near Chicago, Illinois. The company employs 105 workers and made a profit last year, but just barely. Many other window companies are producing high quality windows and are providing a lot of tough competition.

Mr. Peabody has a difficult decision. To help reduce air pollution in large cities, the federal government wants more passengers to ride in each vehicle. Mr. Peabody's company must prepare a plan to get more of the employees to ride together or use public transportation. Since public transportation is limited, he decides that the two best choices for the company are 1) requiring the workers to pay a $10 per week parking fee or 2) giving a carpooling "bonus" of $5 per week to workers who carpool.

Most of the workers, of course, like the idea of getting a $5 bonus for carpooling. Some workers, however, can't carpool because they don't live near any other workers. They don't think it is fair that other workers should get the bonus. Also, Mr. Peabody isn't sure the company can afford the bonus. "If I give the carpooling bonus, I won't be able to give my employees a pay raise next year," he explains. None of the workers like the idea of the parking fee, but Mr. Peabody explains that this is probably the best way to get workers to carpool. It also would help the company to make more profits. This probably will mean more pay raises for workers, and it will mean that workers have a better chance of keeping their jobs. "If the company's production costs continue to go up, "said Mr. Peabody, "some workers will be laid off."

The company must tell the government its plan by next week. What do you think the company should do?

# The Case of the Company Carpool

**Step 1: Define the Problem:** What kind of transportation plan should be implemented?

**Step 2: List Alternative Solutions:** The two alternatives identified in the case study are 1. Implement a parking fee 2. Give carpool bonuses.

**Step 3: List Important Criteria:** Good points about the parking fee are: helps environment by increasing carpooling, helps keep company profitable so workers can keep jobs and maybe get pay raises. Bad points are: workers don't like it, unfair to workers who cannot carpool.

Good points about the carpool bonus are: helps environment by increasing carpooling, most workers like the idea, rewards workers who carpool. Bad points are: unfair to some workers who can't carpool, reduction in company profits resulting in no wage increases and possible layoffs.

**Step 4: Evaluate Alternative Solutions:** The final decision depends on how students evaluate the good and bad points of each alternative. In this case study, the best alternative for Mr. Peabody is probably the parking fee. For most (but not all) of the workers, the carpooling bonus is the preferred alternative. One thing is sure, not everybody will be happy with the final decision.

# Decision Tree

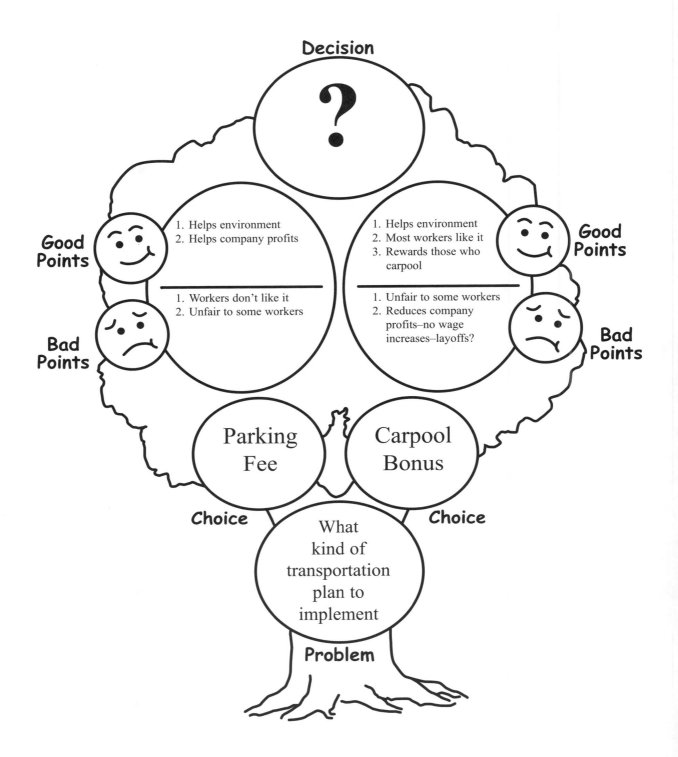

Decision

?

Good Points

1. Helps environment
2. Helps company profits

1. Workers don't like it
2. Unfair to some workers

Good Points

1. Helps environment
2. Most workers like it
3. Rewards those who carpool

1. Unfair to some workers
2. Reduces company profits–no wage increases–layoffs?

Bad Points

Bad Points

Parking Fee

Carpool Bonus

Choice

Choice

What kind of transportation plan to implement

Problem

# The Case of the Company Carpool

1.  **Define the Problem:**  What kind of transportation plan should be implemented?

2.  **List the Alternatives:**  The two alternatives identified in the case study are 1. Implement a parking fee and 2. Give carpooling bonuses.

3.  **List Important Criteria:**  Some important criteria are:  effect on environment, effect on wages and employment, effect on company profits, workers' acceptance of the plan, and fairness.  Students may want to use other criteria.

4.  **Evaluate the Alternative Solutions:**  This is the most challenging part of the problem.  Students put a plus in each cell of the Decision-Making Grid if the criterion "fits" the alternative.  A minus is placed in a cell if the alternative does not "fit." Students put a question mark if the "fit" is neutral or indeterminate.  Below is how a decision grid could be completed in this case study.  Be prepared for students to disagree on the cell markings.

5.  **Choose the Best Alternative (Make a Decision!):**  The final decision will depend on how well the criteria "fit" the alternatives.  The final decision will also depend on how students weigh (value) the criteria.  Students can weight the criteria by circling the one or two criteria they think are most important.  In this case study, the best alternative for Mr. Peabody is probably the parking fee.  For most of the workers, the carpooling bonus is the preferred alternative.  One thing is sure, not everybody will be happy with the final decision!

## Decision-Making Grid Answer Key
## The Case of the Company Carpool

| Criteria | | | | | |
| --- | --- | --- | --- | --- | --- |
| **Alternatives** | **effect on environment** | **effect on wages and jobs** | **effect on company profits** | **workers' acceptance of plan** | **fairness** |
| **$10 Parking Fee** | + | + | + | - | ? |
| **$5 Carpool Bonus** | + | - | - | + | ? |

# Unit 1

## Basic Economic Concepts

# Overview of Unit 1

## Basic Economic Concepts

### Introduction:

One of the main purposes of this *Energy, Economics, and the Environment (EEE)* curriculum is to help students understand the economic implications of basic public policy issues concerning forests, water, and energy. Unit 1 teaches the basic economic concepts that students should know to be able to do Units 2-4 effectively. The key concepts are **goods** and **services, productive resources, scarcity, opportunity cost, trade-offs, and price.**

In each activity in this unit, students use play dough to help them learn the economic concepts. These motivating activities are adaptations of lessons found in the popular *Play Dough Economics* curriculum published by the Indiana Department of Education and distributed by the National Council on Economic Education (NCEE). See www.ncee.net.

An optional curriculum that can be used with this unit is the five-part *Econ and Me* video series, produced by the Agency for Instructional Technology and the NCEE. Using these videos to teach the economic concepts presented in this unit is not required, but will help those teachers who are not confident about their knowledge of basic economics. *Econ and Me* also teaches students how to use the Decision Tree model, which is used throughout this curriculum. For ordering information see www.ncee.net.

### Learning Objectives:

After completing Unit 1, students will be able to:

1.  Understand and apply the economic concepts of goods and services, productive resources, scarcity, opportunity cost, trade-offs, and price.

2.  Analyze a problem using a decision-making model.

### Unit Outline:

    I.   Teaching Activities

        1.  Goods and Services
        2.  Resources and Production
        3.  Scarcity
        4.  Opportunity Cost and Trade-Offs: Focus on Consumers
        5.  Opportunity Cost and Trade-Offs: Focus on Producers

    II.  Answers to Selected Teaching Activities

    III. Play Dough Recipe

# Activity 1
## Goods and Services

**Teaching Objectives:** After completing this activity, students will be able to:

1. Explain that goods and services are things that people want.
2. Identify the difference between a good and a service.

**Time Allowed:**  30-40 minutes

**Materials:**
- Enough play dough for each student to produce a small sculpture
- Examples of goods
- Pictures showing people performing services

**Vocabulary/Concepts:**

- *Goods:* tangible items that satisfy peoples' wants, such as shirts, automobiles, wooden boards, gasoline, or paper.

- *Services:* nonphysical results of production, activities that satisfy people's wants. They are consumed as soon as they are produced. Examples include the services of a dentist, trash collector, or utility company.

Goods are, by definition, things that people want, and people typically must pay to get them. Items that people do not want are **garbage** or **trash.** People have to pay to get *rid* of these! Some recyclable materials, such as aluminum, command a positive **market price,** and could be considered goods.

**Teaching Procedure:**

1. Explain that all individuals want to have a wide variety of things. Ask students to identify things they would like to have. Write these things in a "wishing well" that you draw on the board or on the overhead.

2. Discuss the students' wishes. Discuss other more mundane wants that people have. Explain that the tangible things that people produce to satisfy wants are called **goods.**

3. Explain that **services** are also things that people want. Teach this difference, showing pictures of people performing services. Let some students pretend to be performing some service, and let the other students try to guess what it is.

4. Pass out enough play dough for each student to make a small **good.** Allow five to eight minutes to produce the goods. Go around the room and examine each student's work. Let each student describe his or her work. Discuss whether the items are indeed goods.

5. Repeat the exercise. This time tell students to produce a play dough sculpture of someone performing a **service.** Discuss the services the students produced.

6. Have students complete the Goods and Services worksheet. Discuss student responses.

## Teaching Tips:

1. You will want to lay the groundwork for this and other lessons. Some possible rules: use the entire piece of play dough to make the good, keep the play dough on the desk, and don't play with the play dough as the teacher discusses the lesson.

2. The goods the students produce will probably focus on toys, candy, pets, etc. Explain that more mundane things (clothes, tools, paper, spoons, etc.) are also things that people want.

## Key Questions to Ask Students:

1. What is a good? *(a tangible item that people want)*

2. What is a service? *(activities that satisfy people's wants)*

3. What do your parents produce — goods or services? *(Answers will vary.)*

4. What do you want to produce when you grow up — a good or service?
   *(Answers will vary.)*

## Bulletin Board Ideas:

1. Draw or make a "wishing well." Have students put their wishes in it and identify whether these wishes are a good or involve a service.

2. Divide the bulletin board into two columns, one for goods and one for services. On 3 x 5 cards, write names or put pictures of goods and services, especially those that relate to energy and the environment. Examples are coal, trash collector, oil, wood, aluminum cans, electrical pipe repair person, water meter reader, oil pipeline repair person. Classify the examples and place into the correct column. Have students find other examples.

## Student Journal Ideas:

1. After the play dough activity, finish this sentence: "Today I learned that ...."

2. Collect or draw pictures of different goods or services.

3. Write a paragraph telling what good or service you want to provide when you grow up.

# Goods and Services

1.   Draw a picture of a **good** and a picture of someone doing a **service.**

2.   In the blanks put G if the item is a GOOD, put S if the item is a SERVICE, and put N if it is **NEITHER** a good or a service.

| | | |
|---|---|---|
| _____ haircut | _____ apple | _____ teaching students |
| _____ garbage | _____ gold | _____ wood boards |
| _____ recycling truck | _____ collecting trash | _____ fixing electric wires |
| _____ paper cup | _____ trash | _____ trash bin |
| _____ oil pipe | _____ fixing an oil pipe | _____ gas meter |

3.   Write a paragraph telling what **good** or **service** you want to provide when you grow up. Tell *why* you want to provide that good or service.  Who would want your good or service?

_____

_____

_____

_____

# Activity 2
## Resources and Production

---

**Teaching Objectives:** After completing this activity, students will be able to:

1. Explain that goods and services must be produced.
2. List the three basic categories of productive resources.
3. Give examples of natural resources (land), human resources (labor), and capital resources.
4. Diagram the basic Production Model.
5. Explain how energy is required in all production and consumption.
6. Explain how production and consumption will necessarily affect the environment.

**Time Allowed:**  Two 30 - 40 minute periods

**Materials:**
- A small amount of play dough for each student
- Pencils, ruler, scissors, and other "capital resources"
  (Optional: *Econ and Me* video 4 — "Production")

## Vocabulary/Concepts:

- *Productive Resources:*  the inputs (natural, human, and capital) used to produce goods and services.

- *Production:*  combining productive resources to obtain goods and services.

- *Natural Resources:*  resources found in nature which are used in production, such as air, water, trees, or the land itself.

- *Human Resources:*  the people who work to produce goods and services.

- *Capital Resources:*  special goods, such as buildings, tools, equipment, and machinery, which are used to produce *other* goods and services. Human skills gained through education and training are referred to as *human capital.*

- *Energy Resources:*  resources such as oil, natural gas, uranium, and coal.

**Producers** (entrepreneurs) take the initiative to purchase **productive resources** (inputs) and use them to produce the goods and services (output) they think **consumers** will purchase. Producers are seeking to make a **profit.**

All production and consumption require the use of some form of **energy.**  All production and consumption also pollutes the environment to some degree.  This unavoidable effect isn't all bad since societies must have goods and services to survive and prosper.  Societies must choose how much pollution they are willing to tolerate. Zero pollution is impossible.

## Teaching Procedure:

If you decide to explore the topic of production in more depth, this lesson can be expanded significantly. There are many creative activities that your students can do.

1.  To introduce this lesson, ask students to recall from Lesson 1 some of the different **goods** and **services** that people want. Ask how people get these goods and services. *(Businesses produce them. The goods are then transported by truck, rail, etc., to the stores. Transportation costs are built in to the price of the goods.)*

2.  Explain and discuss the difference between a **producer** and a **consumer.**

3.  Explain that businesses use **productive resources** to produce goods and services. Use actual examples and/or pictures of the three types of productive resources and explain the differences between them. Use the Production Model below in your discussion.

Figure 1

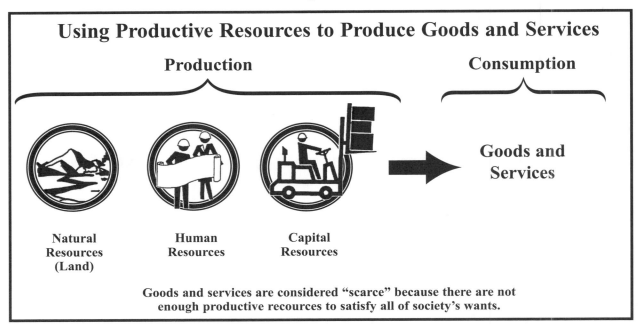

**Using Productive Resources to Produce Goods and Services**

Production                                    Consumption

Natural          Human          Capital                    Goods and
Resources        Resources      Resources                  Services
(Land)

Goods and services are considered "scarce" because there are not
enough productive recources to satisfy all of society's wants.

4.  Ask students to produce a **good** using play dough. The play dough represents the **natural resources,** the students represent **human resources,** and any small "tool" (pencil, ruler, scissors, desk, etc.) represents **capital resources.** Students can use their "capital" to help fashion their good or to make designs and marks that make it look more realistic.

5.  Discuss student creations. Have several students identify the **productive resources** that would be necessary to produce a real good. Write these on the board.

6.  (Optional) Show and discuss *Econ and Me* video 4 — "Production."

7.  Have students complete Handout 1. Discuss student responses.

8.  Discuss the **energy** that is required to produce various **goods** and **services** (Figure 2, page 6). Also discuss how all production and consumption results in some pollution of the environment (Figure 3, page 7). Have students complete worksheet 2. Discuss student responses.

## Teaching Tips:

1. Make a point to identify productive resources when they appear in stories, textbooks, and classroom discussion. As you learn to use the term more frequently, your students will learn it naturally and will begin to use it themselves.

2. Emphasize that the "capital" (pencils, rulers, desk, etc.) your students use in production represents real tools, machinery, buildings, and equipment that businesses use.

## Key Questions to Ask Students:

1. Where do goods and services come from? *(They must be produced.)*

2. What is the difference between a producer and a consumer? *(Producers make goods and services; consumers buy and use goods and services.)*

3. What are productive resources? *(basic things we need to produce goods and services)*

4. What are the three basic types of productive resources? *(natural, human, capital)*

5. What are examples of the different types of productive resources? *(answers will vary)*

6. What are some examples of energy resources? *(oil, natural gas, uranium, coal, etc.)*

7. Is energy always necessary when we produce and consume goods and services? *(yes)*

8. Does production and consumption always result in some pollution? *(yes)*

9. Can a community ever have zero pollution? *(no)*

## Bulletin Board Ideas:

1. Divide the bulletin board into three columns. Cut out pictures from magazines and classify them in three columns labeled natural, human, and capital resources.

2. Create a bulletin board for each of the productive resources.

3. Create a bulletin board titled "Our Energy Resources."

4. Illustrate and label the basic production model. Add to the model by showing a. how energy is needed for production and consumption (Figure 2, page 6) and b. how the wastes of production consumption impact the environment and other people (Figure 3, page 7) , (Figure 5, page 11).

## Student Journal Ideas:

1. After the play dough activity, finish this sentence: "Today I learned that ...."

2. List and classify what productive resources are needed to produce teaching services.

3. List what types of *energy* are needed for your school.

4. Identify the different types of pollution resulting from a day in your school.

5. Draw and label the basic production model.

# Productive Resources - Handout 1

1. Draw and color a picture of someone performing a **service.**

2. Define **productive resources** _____

   _____

   _____

3. In the blanks below, list some **productive resources** that would be needed to provide the
   service you drew above.

   | Natural Resources | Human Resources | Capital Resources |
   | --- | --- | --- |
   | _____ | _____ | _____ |
   | _____ | _____ | _____ |

4. In the space below, diagram the **production model.** Be sure to label the parts of
   the model.

## The Production Model

# Productive Resources - Handout 2

1.  Draw and color a picture of someone producing a good.

2.  List three different kinds of **energy** needed in the production you drew above.

    _____     _____     _____

3.  List four kinds of **pollution** or **waste** that come from the production you drew above.

    _____     _____

    _____     _____

4.  Make four small drawings that show how you use energy in your home.

5.  List three different kinds of **pollution** or **waste** that come from your home.

    _____     _____     _____

6.  Is it possible to eliminate *all* the pollution from the production of the good above?

    _____

7.  Is it possible to eliminate *all* the pollution that comes from your home? _____

8.  In your drawing in question 1, you could eliminate pollution if you stopped production entirely. Do you think this is a good idea? _____ Discuss this option with your class.

# Activity 3
## Scarcity

**Teaching Objectives:** After completing this activity, students will:

1. Identify a scarcity situation.
2. Explain how the price of an item reflects its relative scarcity.
3. Identify things that are not scarce.

**Time Allowed:** 45 minutes

**Materials:**
- Play dough for each student
- Pencils, ruler, scissors, and other small articles of "capital"
- *Econ and Me* video 1 – "Scarcity" (Optional)

**Vocabulary/Concepts:**

- *Scarcity:* the condition of not being able to have all of the goods, services, or productive resources that you want.

- *Price:* the amount people pay to buy a good, service, or productive resource.

- *Relative Scarcity:* the scarcity of one good or service compared to another. The price of a good or service reflects its relative scarcity.

In economics, **scarce** does not necessarily mean "rare." Any item is considered scarce if the want for it exceeds its availability - *at a zero price*. However, some items are *more scarce* than others. Items that are highly valued and more limited in supply are relatively more scarce than those which are less highly valued and more abundant in supply. Differences in **prices,** which measure the exchange value of one good or service compared to another, reflect relative scarcity. This is why a car costs more than a pencil and why sports superstars earn more than teachers or plumbers. The concept of scarcity is so fundamental to economics that it is often called "the basic economic problem."

It is difficult to identify things that are *not* scarce. Examples would be saltwater at the seashore or the air you are breathing now. But even air is scarce to the scuba diver or astronaut and certainly clean air is scarce for the inhabitants of large cities. Trash and garbage are *not* scarce - in fact, we pay to get rid of them! Some recyclable materials, such as aluminum, are scarce in the economic sense because they command a price in the market. Other recyclable materials are less scarce and are worth little or nothing in the market. Certain plastics or newsprint may fit this category, depending on the situation.

## Teaching Procedure:

1. (Optional) Show and discuss the *Econ and Me* video "Scarcity." (This video also teaches the concept of **productive resources,** which is covered in Activity 2.)

2. Display an inexpensive good (pencil, eraser, piece of candy, etc.) to the class. Ask which students would like to have the good — free! Since more than one student will want the good, you have a scarcity situation. (See "Scarcity Rule" described in Teaching Tip 1.)

3. Explain that this good and other goods and services are **scarce** (write on board). Explain the economic concept of **scarcity,** giving other examples.

4. Ask students to identify things that are *not* scarce (air we breath in class, snow in a blizzard, salt water at the beach, etc.) Be careful — in certain situations air *is* scarce (underwater, outer space). *Clean air* is scarce in smoggy cities. Explain that garbage and trash are *not* scarce. We must even pay to get *rid* of them!

5. Hand out some play dough to each student. Students must create a scarcity situation showing more than one person wanting a specific, scarce good. Allow about 10 minutes to create sculptures. Give some suggestions. Walk around the room, encouraging students in their work.

6. Have each student explain how his or her sculpture illustrates a scarcity situation. (Does it fit the "Scarcity Rule?")

7. Write "scarce" or "scarcity" on the board and practice spelling it with the students. Have students write and define the word in their journal.

8. Have students do the Scarcity worksheet. Discuss student answers.

## Teaching Tips:

1. The "Scarcity Rule": A simple rule to help students determine whether an item is scarce is this: If the item is made *freely* available, does more than one person want it? If the answer is "yes," then the item is considered scarce. For example, if a teacher offers a free pencil to her class, more than one student will want it. In this situation, the pencil is scarce. If a piece of gold were offered, the same thing would happen. However, if students are freely offered a pencil or the gold, most will choose the gold. In economics *both* items are considered scarce, but gold is relatively *more* scarce, and thus commands a higher price.

2. Do not expect all of your students to master the concept of scarcity the first time. It's not that easy! However, if you use daily situations in your classroom to illustrate the concept ("Six students want the playground ball. It certainly is scarce!") and if you use the concept in the following energy and environmental units, most of your students will master it.

3. If time permits, use some of the teaching activities in the *Econ and Me* teachers manual.

## Key Questions to Ask Students:

1. Give an example of a scarcity situation. *(Answers will vary.)*

2. Give an example of something that is not scarce. *(saltwater at the beach, air in the atmosphere, garbage)*

3. Why isn't garbage or trash considered scarce? *(Nobody wants it. We pay to get rid of it!)*

4. Why are all goods sold in a store scarce? *(At a zero price there would not be enough to satisfy everyone's want for them. The price of goods helps determine who gets them.)*

5. What are some examples of some services that are scarce? *(doctor, nurse, car repair, etc.)*

6. Are energy resources scarce? Why? *(Yes. They are not freely available. It takes scarce productive resources to produce energy.)*

7. In a store, what is the "clue" that tells us which goods are more scarce than others? *(the price of the goods)*

8. Why do athletic superstars make more money than your teacher? *(Their skills are relatively more scarce than the skills of your teacher. Team owners are willing to pay superstars huge salaries since their relatively scarce skills will make money for the team.)*

## Bulletin Board Ideas:

1. Divide the bulletin board into two columns showing scarce goods and scarce services. Also indicate those that are "very scarce" and those that are "not very scarce." Or, divide the bulletin board into two columns, one showing scarce goods and services and the other showing things that are *not* scarce.

2. Create a bulletin board illustrating the "Scarcity Rule" (Teaching Tip 1).

3. Create a bulletin board showing scarce energy resources.

4. Create a bulletin board showing recyclable materials that are scarce (e.g., that have a price in the market, like aluminum) and those that may not be scarce (e.g., like some plastics). Students will have to research the market price of recyclable materials in their region. See Recycler's World – www.recycle.net

## Student Journal Ideas:

1. After the play dough activity, finish this sentence: "Today I learned that ...."
2. Draw a scarcity situation.
3. List and describe scarce energy resources.
4. List items that are "very scarce" and those that are "not very scarce."
5. Write a paragraph explaining why some recyclable materials are considered "scarce" and some are not.
6. Write a paragraph explaining why garbage and trash are *not* scarce.

# Scarcity

1. Draw a **scarcity** situation in the space below.

2. Draw a circle around the items below that are *not* scarce.

   Shirt              Garbage           Automobile            Sand in the desert

   Book               Gold              Air you are breathing    A nurse's services

   TV repair          Shoes             Air in space          Saltwater at the seashore

3. In a store, what "clue" tells you if some item is more scarce than another item?

   _____

   _____

4. Draw a picture of a good that is very scarce and a good that is <u>not</u> very scarce.

5. List four **energy resources**. Are these resources **scarce**? Why? _____

   _____

   _____

   _____

   _____

# Activity 4
## Opportunity Cost and Trade-Offs

*Focus on Consumers*

**Teaching Objectives:**  After completing this activity, students will be able to:

1.    Define and explain opportunity cost.

2.    Identify the opportunity cost of a consumer decision.

3.    Explain why there is an opportunity cost to every consumer decision.

4.    Identify trade-offs when making decisions.

5.    Solve a problem using a decision model.

**Time Allowed**:    Two 30-40 minute periods

**Materials**:
- (Optional) Econ and Me video 2 – "Opportunity Cost"
- A small piece of play dough for each student
- Decision Tree worksheet (page 20)

**Vocabulary/Concepts:**

- *Opportunity Cost:*  the value of the best alternative given up when making a decision.

- *Trade-offs:*  getting a little less of one thing in order to get a little more of another.

Because of **scarcity,** people cannot have everything they want.  They must choose which **goods** and **services** they wish to purchase.  When **consumers** purchase a good or service, they are giving up the chance to purchase another.  The best single alternative not chosen is called the **opportunity cost.**  Since a consumer choice always involves alternatives, every consumer choice has an opportunity cost.

Choices also involve **trade-offs** — getting a little less of one thing in order to get a little more of another.  For example, suppose Mr. Jones decides to extend his vacation trip to Florida from one to two weeks.  This extra cost means not upgrading his computer system, which he really wants to do. In this case, he is trading off better computing capabilities for more vacation time.

**Teaching Procedure:**

1.    (Optional) Show and discuss the *Econ and Me* video, "Opportunity Cost."  Ask students if they would like to do a play dough activity that will help them master this concept.

2.    Ask students if they have ever purchased something at a store.  Tell them that they are going to have a store in their classroom.  Identify a table in the front of the classroom to serve as a "store."  Point out one major problem — the store has no products!  Ask students if they would like to produce some products.

3. Tell students that they first will be **producers.** Briefly explain this concept. Pass out a small amount of play dough to each student. Tell students to use their **productive resources** (natural, human, capital) to produce a **scarce** good that they might find in a typical department store. Tell them to do good work, since their goods will be sold at the class store.

4. After 10 - 15 minutes let each child describe his or her product and then place it in the store.

5. Tell students they will now be **consumers.** Briefly explain this concept. Ask for a volunteer to "shop" at the store. The volunteer must prefer at least two of the other goods to the one he has produced. Choose a student and have him identify the good he produced. Then ask the student to identify the two goods produced by other classmates that he *most* wants and would be willing to trade for. Place these two goods on the store "counter" (a nearby desk). The student must trade his good for one of those two goods. Identify the good *not* purchased as the student's opportunity cost. Ask, "What would be the opportunity cost if he chose the other good instead?" (The good *not* chosen.)

6. Then ask the class to explain the trade-offs of this choice. (If the student traded a baseball bat for some candy, he was trading off baseball recreational opportunities for the benefits of the candy.)

7. After several students have "shopped" at the store, change the rules somewhat. Ask the shoppers to identify three goods that they want most and would be willing to trade for. The opportunity cost will be the one good that was their second choice. (See Teaching Tip 1.)

8. Have students do the Opportunity Cost — Consumers worksheet. Then use the Decision Tree worksheet to solve the two case studies. Discuss student responses.

## Teaching Tips:

1. Students frequently think that the *sum* of their various alternatives is their opportunity cost. This is incorrect since only their next best choice is what is finally given up. For example, suppose Mary is willing and able to purchase choices A, B, or C, in that order of preference. If she purchases A, choice B is her opportunity cost, not B and C.

2. Make sure students understand that the good they trade is not their opportunity cost. Rather, their second choice from the goods they want to trade for is their opportunity cost. Likewise, in a real store, one's opportunity cost is not the money paid for a good, but the next best alternative good that was not purchased!

## Key Questions to Ask Students:

1. If I have two choices A and B, and I purchase B, what is my opportunity cost? (*choice A*)

2. Suppose I have three consumer choices A, B, and C, and each costs $10. If I purchase B, why aren't both A and C my opportunity cost? (*I cannot purchase both A and C. I am really giving up only my second best choice.*)

3. Why is there an opportunity cost to every decision? (*There is always an alternative choice that was given up.*)

4. Sally has enough money to buy two new pens for school. She wants both pens, but decides instead to purchase one pen and one piece of candy. What is her trade-off? (*She is trading off the benefits of an extra pen to get candy.*)

5. A city uses its tax money to purchase a recycling truck instead of making a new park. What is the trade-off? (*The city is trading off park services for recycling services.*)

## Bulletin Board Ideas:

1. Show the opportunity cost and/or trade-offs of various choice situations, such as the city's recycling/park situation in Key Question 5 above.

2. Show the Decision Tree (from the *Econ and Me* video) being used to solve a problem. Identify the opportunity cost of the decision.

## Student Journal Ideas:

1. After the play dough activity, finish this sentence: "Today I learned that ...."

2. Draw an opportunity cost situation. Write a sentence explaining the diagram.

3. Describe a choice you had to make. Identify the opportunity cost of the choice.

4. Write a paragraph describing a choice a city might have to make. What are the pros and cons of the possible choices? What is the opportunity cost of the final decision? Draw a picture that goes with the paragraph.

# Opportunity Cost — Consumers

1. In your own words, write what **opportunity cost** means.

   _____
   _____

2. You have just received $10 for a birthday present from your uncle. You want to spend it on either a soccer ball, a large box of candy, or a new shirt. (Each costs $10.) Put a 1 under your first choice, a 2 under your second choice, and a 3 under your third choice.

   _____        _____        _____

3. What is the **opportunity cost** of your first choice? _____

4. Were your choices the same as those of your classmates? _____
   Why not? _____
   _____

5. Suppose your friend has the same first choice as you. Does this mean his or her **opportunity cost** is the same as yours? Why or why not? _____
   _____
   _____
   _____
   _____

6. Sara has one hour until bedtime. She can take a walk, play a game, or bake a cake. She decides to play a game. Her second choice is to take a walk, and her third choice is to bake a cake.

   a. What is the **opportunity cost** of her decision to play a game? _____

   b. Can Sara's opportunity cost be taking a walk *and* baking a cake? _____
      Why or why not? _____
      _____
      _____
      _____

# Case Studies

**Directions:** Work in groups. Use the Decision Tree to help you decide what to do in the two case studies below.

---

**Case Study 1**

Your parents are going to let you invite eight of your friends to a birthday party. After discussing the various alternatives with your parents, your two choices for a party are

- A kickball party followed by a hotdog and marshmallow roast at a local park.
- A miniature golf party followed by pizza at your house.

You really would like to do both, but it's not possible. Half of your friends want the kickball party while half want the miniature golf party. You just don't know what to do!

---

1. Which birthday party will you choose? _____

2. What is the **opportunity cost** of your choice? _____

---

**Case Study 2**

Your city has $20,000 of tax money to use to make your city a better place to live. The city council has narrowed the possibilities down to the two choices described below. The decision must be made next week.

- Use the tax money to plant 300 new trees along some streets of the city. This will provide more shade, make the city more beautiful, and give animals, such as squirrels and birds, more places to live.

- Use the money to build another baseball/softball field for the children of the city. Right now there are just too many teams for the one existing field. Some of the children cannot be on a team because there is no place to play games if more teams are formed.

---

1. What would you do? _____

What is the **opportunity cost** of your decision? If the city selects your decision, what **trade-offs** would the city be making? _____

_____

_____

# Activity 5
## Opportunity Cost and Trade-Offs

*Focus on Producers*

---

**Teaching Objectives:** After completing this activity, students will be able to:

1. Define and explain opportunity cost.
2. Identify the cost of producer decisions.
3. Explain why there is a cost to every producer decision.
4. Identify trade-offs when making decisions.
5. Solve a problem using a decision model.

**Time Allowed:**  Two 30 – 50 minute periods

**Materials:**
- A small piece of play dough for each student
- (Optional) *Econ and Me* video #4 — "Production"
- Opportunity Cost and Case Study Worksheets

## Vocabulary/Concepts

- *Opportunity Cost:*  the value of the best alternative given up when making a decision.

- *Trade-off:*  getting a little less of one thing in order to get a little more of another.

**Producers** use **productive resources** to produce **goods** and services.  Because productive resources are **scarce,** there are not enough to produce all of the goods and services that people want.  Producers must **choose** which goods and services to produce.  Productive resources used to produce one good or service cannot be used to produce another.  For example, a producer cannot use the same building (capital resource) for a pizza restaurant and an insurance agency.

The single most valuable opportunity given up when a producer makes a decision is the **opportunity cost.**  Suppose a pizza restaurant and an insurance business are the best uses for a particular building.  If a producer decides to use the building for a pizza restaurant, *not* being able to use it for an insurance business would be the opportunity cost.  The opportunity cost of choosing to use the building as an insurance agency would be the lost benefits of using it for a pizza restaurant.

Producer decisions also involve **trade-offs** — getting a little more of one option in exchange for a little less of another.  If a community government decides to use limited tax revenues to build more parks and fewer roads, the government is trading off roads for parks.

## Teaching Procedure:

1. (Optional) Show and discuss *Econ and Me* video 4 — "Production." Tell students they will do a play dough activity that will help them learn more about production and opportunity cost.

2. Tell students that they will be **producers** in this activity in order to learn more about **opportunity cost.** Distribute a small amount of play dough to each student. Ask them to use their **productive resources** (natural, human, and capital) to produce one of two types of goods: something to *eat* (food) or something to *wear* (clothing).

3. After 6-10 minutes, collect and admire the finished products. Place them on a table in front of the room.

4. Have students count how many items of food and clothing have been produced. List the number on the board.

| | Food | Clothing |
|---|---|---|
| Example: | 11 | 9 |

5. Tell the class that they may want to make some changes in what was produced. Perhaps they would like to have more food or more clothing. Take a vote to determine if the class would like more food or more clothing. In this example, assume that the class votes for more food.

6. Choose one of the more "artistic" clothing items and slowly and deliberately crush and mold it into a crude food item (apple, pancake, etc.). Repeat this with two other clothing items. As the class moans and groans, tell them that you are only doing what it wanted — producing more food!

7. After you have finished, announce that the class is definitely better off now since there is more food. Wait a few moments. Hopefully, a perceptive student will respond, "Not necessarily. Now we don't have as much clothing!" Explain that because there is a **scarcity** of productive resources, there is an **opportunity cost** to getting the extra food. Ask the class to identify the opportunity cost (two clothing items). Students should understand that the opportunity cost for producers are the goods or services *not* produced as a result of producing something else.

8. Discuss the concept of **trade-offs.** Explain that the class was trading off clothing to get more food. Emphasize that many decisions are not all or nothing. We frequently accept less of one thing in order to get more of another.

9. Have students do the Opportunity Cost — Producers worksheet and the Case Study. Discuss student responses.

## Teaching Tips:

1. Students will often produce food instead of clothing. For the teaching activity to be successful, a sufficient number of both items needs to be produced. Before students begin, it is helpful to mention various clothing items (shoes, rings, necklaces, hats, etc.) that they could produce.

2.  You should explain that over time more food *and* clothing can be produced, especially as productivity increases. This certainly has been the case in the United States during the past two centuries. But at any one point in time, producing more food means producing less clothing (assuming that food and clothing are the only goods produced).

3.  This is an important lesson because most lessons on opportunity cost focus only on consumer choice. Few lessons emphasize that producers also must make choices that have opportunity costs.

## Key Questions to Ask Students:

1.  Give an example of a producer having to make choices. (*Answers will vary. Producers must choose what to produce and how to produce it.*)

2.  What does opportunity cost mean? (*the best alternative you must give up to get something else*)

3.  Sally must decide what to do when she grows up. She wants to be a nurse or an accountant, but unfortunately she cannot be both. What is her opportunity cost if she decides to be an accountant? (*being a nurse*) What is her opportunity cost if she decides to become a nurse? (*being an accountant*)

4.  Why is there an opportunity cost to every producer decision? (*There are always other production alternatives that can be chosen.*)

5.  A clothing producer uses his productive resources to produce more blue jeans and fewer T-shirts. What is the trade-off? (*The producer is trading off T-shirts for blue jeans.*)

6.  Why might a producer decide to produce more blue jeans and fewer T-shirts? (*Producing blue jeans might bring more profit for the producer.*)

## Bulletin Board Ideas:

1.  Show the opportunity cost of a producer decision (a farmer choosing to produce corn instead of wheat, etc.).

2.  Show the opportunity cost of choosing a certain career.

## Student Journal Ideas:

1.  After the play dough activity, finish the sentence: "Today I learned that ...."
2.  Draw a producer opportunity cost situation. Write a sentence explaining the diagram.
3.  Write a paragraph describing what you might like to be when you grow up. In your paragraph, list several things you might like to do and identify the opportunity cost of a career decision.

# Opportunity Cost - Producers

1.  What is the difference between a **producer** and a **consumer?** Give some examples of each.

    _____

    _____

    _____

    _____

2.  Write the **opportunity cost** of each decision in the blanks.

    a.  Last year Farmer Smith planted 20 acres of corn and 20 acres of soybeans on his 40-acre farm.  This year he planted 30 acres of corn and 10 acres of soybeans.  _____

        _____

    b.  Mrs. Johnson wants to use her vacant building to operate either a pizza restaurant or an insurance business.  She decides to operate the pizza restaurant.  _____

        _____

    c.  Mr. Williams teaches 5th grade science.  He has only one week left in the school year.  He wants to teach a unit on water resources and a unit on insects, but he does not have time to do both.  He decides to teach the unit on water.  _____

        _____

    d.  Sarah must decide what to study when she goes to college.  She wants to be either a lawyer, a teacher, or an actress.  She decides to be a teacher. Her second choice was to be a lawyer, and her third choice was to be an actress.

        _____

3.  Draw a picture showing a **producer** having to choose between two alternatives.  In the picture, identify the **opportunity cost.**  Below the picture, write a short paragraph explaining the decision and the opportunity cost.

# Case Study

**Directions:** Work in groups. Decide what Sam should do in this case study. In the space below, draw a Decision Tree or a Decision Grid to help your group come to a decision.

---

Sam is very perplexed! He must decide what to do when he graduates from college. He has studied forestry and really likes growing and taking care of forests and trees. His father has some land nearby that Sam can use to develop a tree farm. He would be the manager of the farm and would make all of the important decisions. However, a large tree company has offered him a good job taking care of forests in Oregon. It is a job he really likes, and the pay is better than what he would earn developing his father's land. However, he wouldn't be the "boss" and wouldn't make nearly as many decisions himself if he worked for the company. He also would have to move far away from his family. What should Sam do?

---

Which job do you think Sam should take? _____

What is the **opportunity cost** of the decision you made for Sam?

_____

_____

What are some of the **trade-offs** Sam is making if he does what your group decided?

_____

_____

Put Decision Tree or Decision Grid Here or on the back.

# Answers to Selected Teaching Activities

**Activity 1:** **Goods and Services Handout:** 2. *Goods:* recycling truck, paper cup, oil pipe, apple, gold, wood boards, trash bin, gas meter. *Services:* haircut, collecting trash, fixing an oil pipe, teaching students, fixing electric wires. *Neither:* garbage, trash

**Activity 2:** **Productive Resources Handout:** 2. These are the natural, human, and capital resources needed to produce a good or service. 3. Answers will vary. 4. See Figure 1 on page 5.

**Productive Resources:** Questions 1-5: Answers will vary. 6. No 7. No 8. Probably not. It will depend on the amount, toxicity, etc., of the pollution. Explain that, although production results in some pollution, it also results in valuable goods and services.

**Activity 3:** **Scarcity Handout:** 2. Items that are *not* scarce: garbage, air you are breathing now, sand in the desert, saltwater at the seashore. 3. Items that are relatively more scarce have a higher price. 4. Examples of very scarce goods: diamonds, gold, etc. Examples of not very scarce goods: pencils, paper clips, common baseball cards, etc. 5. Examples include oil, gas, nuclear plants, coal, geothermal systems, wind towers, solar systems, etc. Yes, they are not freely available in unlimited quantities.

**Activity 4:** **Opportunity Cost – Consumers Handout:** 1. When you make a choice, it is the value of your next best alternative. 3. The second choice 4. No. People's values differ 5. No! The second choice, which is the opportunity cost, could differ. 6a. taking a walk. 6b. No. She can't choose to do both at the same time; thus, only her second choice is her opportunity cost.

**Case Studies:** Decisions will vary. In each case study, the opportunity cost is always the alternative not chosen. In Case Study 2, the trade-offs are the recreational benefits for environmental/beautification benefits, or vice versa.

**Activity 5:** **Opportunity Cost – Producers Handout:** 1. Producers make goods and services; consumers buy and use them. 2a. 10 acres of soybeans. b. the benefits of using the building as an insurance business. c. what the students would learn by studying insects. d. being a lawyer.

**Case Study:** The opportunity cost is the alternative not chosen. Sam is trading off the benefits of being his own boss and staying near his family for the benefits of more money.

# PLAY DOUGH RECIPE

| 1 cup flour | 1/2 cup salt | 1 T. oil |
| 1 cup water | 2 t. cream of tartar | food coloring |

Directions: Cook and stir over medium heat until a ball forms. Knead in a large zip-lock bag for a few minutes. Remove air from bag and zip shut. This recipe makes enough play dough to fill an average-sized sandwich bag.

# Unit 2

# Trees and Forests

# Overview of Unit 2

## Trees and Forests

### Introduction:

Trees and forests are a vital natural resource and affect our lives in innumerable ways. Therefore, it is very important that we learn how to manage our forest resource effectively. Fortunately, forest management in the United States has improved greatly since the early part of this century when our forests were often abused. Forest growth is improving steadily, even in the face of increasing demand for wood products. Nevertheless, there is still a need for better forest management, and there are still controversial issues that confront policymakers. Your elementary students will enjoy learning about trees and forests and the difficult public policy issues surrounding them.

### Learning Objectives:

After completing this unit, students will:

1.  Learn to analyze a problem using a decision-making model.
2.  Explain some of the basic benefits of trees and forest resources.
3.  Understand key facts about trees and forest resources in the United States.
4.  Learn to apply the concepts of scarcity, choice, opportunity cost, and price.

### Unit Outline:

I.   Facts About Forests and Forest Management in the United States

II.  Teaching Instructions and Key Concepts to Emphasize

III. Specific Teaching Activities

    1.   Leaves and Trees
    2.   Our Valuable Trees – A Skit
    3.   Forests and Forest Products
    4.   Forest Benefits and Conflicting Goals
    5.   Forest Economics
    6.   Conducting a Forest Survey
    7.   Making Recycled Paper
    8.   Further Explorations
    9.   Let's Talk It Over
    10.  EEE Actions – You Can Make a Difference!
    11.  Case Study – "The Case of the Class Field Trip"

IV.  Answers to Selected Teaching Activities

# Facts About Forests and Forest Management
# in the United States

## Introduction

Forest management plays a crucial role in natural resource conservation. Our forests are important for many reasons, and issues concerning the management of our forests have received much attention in recent years. Wise public policy decisions concerning our forests require citizens and decision makers who are knowledgeable about basic forest facts and forest management.

## Benefits of Our Forests

A **forest** is a dynamic community composed of living and nonliving things which is dominated by trees. Forests provide enormous and diverse benefits to our society and world. Indeed, to sustain a lifestyle beyond a bare subsistence level, forest resources are virtually a necessity. The basic benefits forest resources provide are categorized below into five major groups.

### Group 1: Forest Products

Forest products are used in an estimated 5,000 commercial products, mainly comprised of lumber, paper, and plywood. However, trees are also used in the production of resins, waxes, medicines, vitamins, adhesives, lacquers, mulches, various chemicals, dinnerware, electrical receptacles, handles for cooking utensils and tools, textile products, baby food, cattle feed, insecticides, printing inks, asphalt, chewing gum, cement, ceramics, fertilizers, cosmetics, gummed tape, and many other items. Other kinds of special forest products include Christmas trees, nuts, and syrup.

Wood is also a primary energy source and is used by many for heating and cooking. Today, about two billion people in the world are dependent on wood fuel for cooking, heating, and food preservation. Worldwide, almost two-thirds of all wood cut is used for fuel. Nationally, over one-half of the paper industry's total energy requirement is met by burning wood residues, such as ground wood, bark, and pulping liquors.

Individuals and businesses who grow, manage, and harvest trees and produce manufactured wood and paper products make up the core of the forest industry, which has annual sales of about $230 billion. It employs about 1.7 million people, with an annual payroll of over $51 billion. In 2000, United States exports of paper, pulp, and wood totaled $18.1 billion. Imports were $30.4 billion. Canada ($5.6 billion) is the largest customer of U.S. wood and paper products, followed by Mexico ($2.8 billion), the European Union ($2.6 billion), and Japan ($2.3 billion).

With 56,000 workers, Indiana's vibrant forest products industry is the sixth largest employer in Indiana. Hardwood logs are the most important and valuable products, with 95% of Indiana's forests classified as hardwood forest. The industry produced 348 million board feet of saw logs in 2000, up from 289 million board feet in 1995. The most important hardwoods are red and white oak, tulip tree, hickory, ash, and hard maple. Pulpwood production has also grown. The wood residues from sawmills provide 83 percent of all pulpwood.

## Group 2: Outdoor Recreation

Forests are places of tremendous scenic beauty and solitude, and are thus invaluable resources for outdoor recreation. They provide places suitable for bird watching, hiking, camping, hunting, and other recreational activities. Many people have jobs directly or indirectly connected with these recreational pursuits.

## Group 3: Biodiversity and Wildlife Habitat

Home to about two-thirds of all species on earth, forest ecosystems are the world's largest reservoir of biological diversity and are a natural habitat for a wide variety of wildlife. In addition to being a primary food source, forests are sources of cover, giving wildlife protection from adverse weather, concealment for breeding and rearing young, or simply a place to rest.

## Group 4: Watershed Protection

A **watershed** is a major land area that collects and delivers run-off water, sediment, and dissolved substances to rivers and heir tributaries. Forest watersheds can be compared to gigantic sponges which regulate the flow of runoff waters from highland sources to cropland and urban areas. The water absorbed and held by forest watersheds is used to recharge springs, streams, and ground water aquifers. This absorption process helps control soil erosion, flooding, and the amount of sediment flowing into rivers and reservoirs.

## Group 5: Climate Control and Source of Oxygen

Trees and other green plants are the primary source of the oxygen that humans and animals need to survive. The complex chemical process that produces oxygen is called photosynthesis. In photosynthesis, carbon dioxide ($CO_2$) from the atmosphere combines with water ($H_2O$) in the tree leaves. This produces a basic sugar ($C_6H_{12}O_6$) and releases oxygen ($O_2$) to the air. Photosynthesis is catalyzed by chlorophyll and energized by sunlight. The chemical formula is:

$$6\ CO_2\ +\ 6\ H_2O\ +\ Solar\ Energy\ ====>\ C_6H_{12}O_6 + 6\ O_2$$

Young, vigorously growing forests produce vast quantities of oxygen. As forests age, they produce less oxygen. In old, overcrowded forests, more wood may be decaying than is being added by growth. The decaying process may cause these forests to use more oxygen than they produce.

# Forest Resources in the United States

**FOREST ACREAGE**: The United States is blessed with abundant forest resources. One-third of the United States (approximately 747 million acres out of a total land mass of 2.3 billion acres) is forestland. This is about two-thirds of the forest cover that existed in 1600. To be classified as forestland, an area must be at least one acre in size and contain at least 10 percent tree cover.

Of the 747 million acres of forestland, 504 million acres are classified as timberland, forests capable of growing at least 20 cubic feet of commercial wood per acre per year. Approximately 51 million acres of this timberland are reserved forests. These acres have been set aside from any timber harvesting by law under the National Wilderness System and also include National and State parks. The remaining 453 million acres are classified as commercial timberland, land that is available and suitable for growing and harvesting trees. Most (58%) commercial timberland is private land. Of the rest, 29% is owned by federal, state, and local governments and 13% is owned by the forest industry. Overall, only about one half of available commercial timberland is actually used for growing and harvesting trees. Portions are often set aside for non-timber uses, such as recreation and wildlife habitat.

Figure 2-1

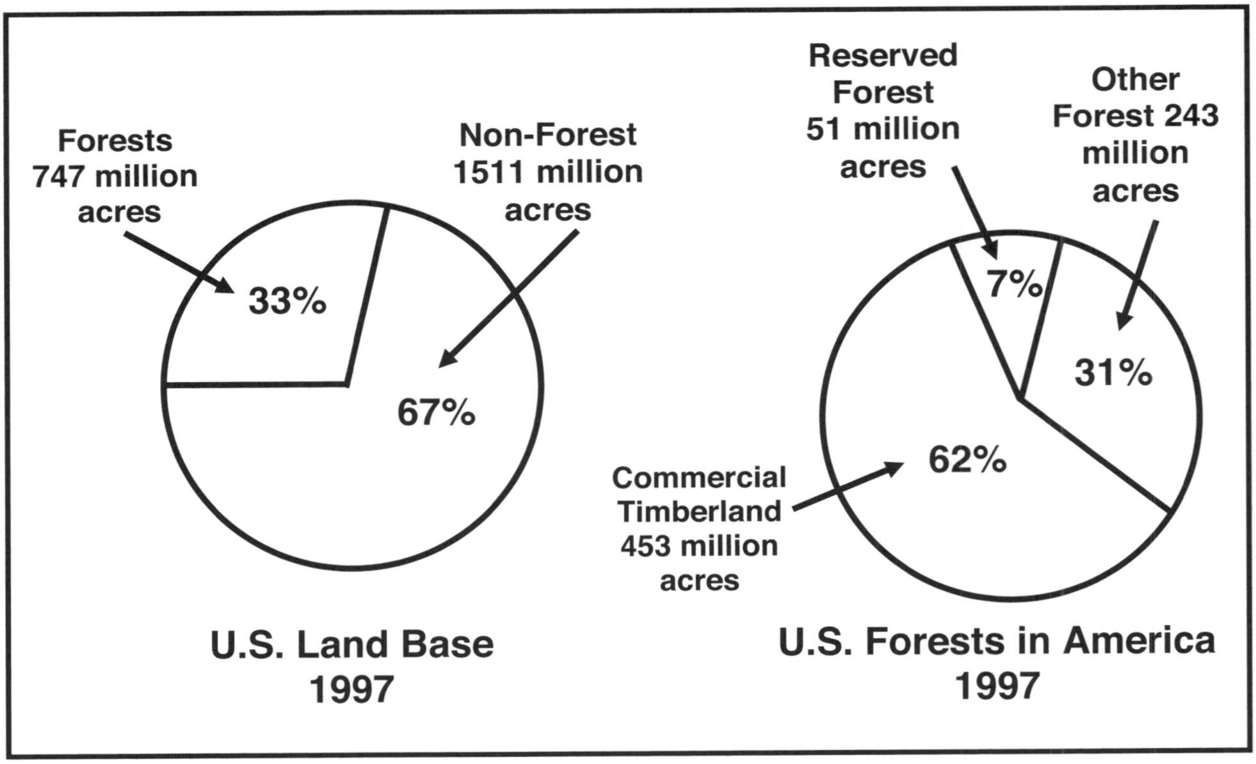

Forests 747 million acres — 33%

Non-Forest 1511 million acres — 67%

**U.S. Land Base 1997**

Reserved Forest 51 million acres — 7%

Other Forest 243 million acres — 31%

Commercial Timberland 453 million acres — 62%

**U.S. Forests in America 1997**

**FOREST OWNERSHIP:** There are three categories of forest ownership in the United States:

1. Public (federal, state, local, and Indian reservations)
2. Private (non-industrial)
3. Private (industrial)

Figure 2-2 shows the breakdown. Public land is a significant portion of our nation's forestland and is managed by various levels of government, with the federal government playing the most significant role. Private non-industrial forests consist primarily of relatively small, individually owned woodland plots. Private industrial forestland is owned by large timber companies.

Figure 2-2

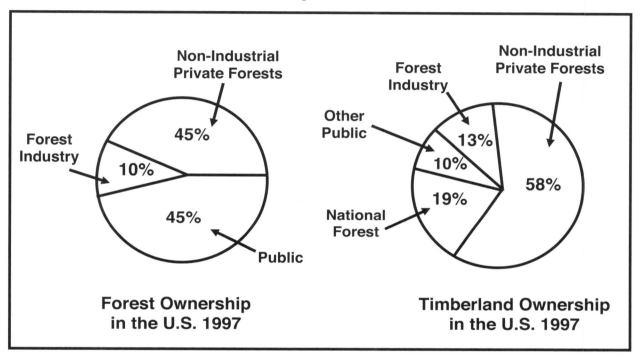

**FEDERAL FORESTLANDS:** The federal government owns a significant portion of our public forestland. A wide variety of regulations and laws guide the use of these lands. Below is a brief summary of federal lands and their use.

*National Forests*: Congress established the national forest system in the late 1800s. National forests now cover about 192 million acres. These are "working forests" created to help ensure a continual supply of wood products. Timber harvesting is permitted on some of the national forests. The U.S. Department of Agriculture's Forest Service manages the national forests under the principle of multiple use. Multiple-use management means that national forests must also protect and enhance the other benefits of our forests, including watershed protection, wildlife habitats, and recreation.

Other federal lands are designated as set-aside areas. The purpose of these areas is to promote noncommercial forest uses, so timber harvesting is prohibited. Various federal agencies now manage over 258 million acres of forested and nonforested set-aside lands.

***Wilderness Lands*:**   The Wilderness Act of 1964 established the National Wilderness System, the largest set-aside program.  Wilderness lands may be forested or unforested, and have no roads, power lines, or other signs of modern civilization.  Today there are more than 106.5 million acres in the Wilderness Preservation System.  Since its creation, the System has grown almost every year.  The passage of the Alaska National Interest Lands Conservation Act added over 56 million acres of wilderness to the System, the greatest increase ever.  Most wilderness lands are in Alaska.

***Fish and Wildlife Land:*** A similar amount of land, 96 million acres, is managed by the U.S. Fish and Wildlife Service. These lands are similar to wilderness lands.  They are set aside as National Wildlife Refuges, Waterfowl Protection Areas, Wildlife Research Areas, Fish Hatcheries, and Fish Research Stations.

***Bureau of Land Management Lands*:**   The Bureau of Land Management oversees over 261.9 million acres. They include Areas of Critical Environmental Concern, Research Natural Areas, Outstanding Natural Areas, National Natural Landmarks, Wilderness Study Areas, and Wilderness Lands.

***National Park Land*:**  Another large set-aside program is the National Park System.  In 1872, Congress established Yellowstone, the world's first national park.  Today, national park lands total 84.4 million acres.  By law, the National Park System has two primary goals:  to conserve the natural scenery and wildlife for future generations, and to let people enjoy the natural beauty of the parks.  The national parks' biggest problem has been their success. Annual usage has increased dramatically over the years, often putting biological stresses on park resources.

# Forest Growth

**OUR GROWING FORESTS:**  While deforestation is a serious concern in many countries, forests in the United States are in no danger of disappearing.  American forests have actually grown in size over the past century, and scientists estimate that our forests now contain 230 billion trees.  In the nation's commercial forests, net annual growth i.e. timber growth minus losses to harvesting, disease, and insects, is growing slowly but steadily - about .2 percent a year.  This growth is partly driven by higher stumpage prices for cut trees due to the large increase in demand for timber products during the past decades, which provides an economic incentive to continually improve the science of forestry.

There are several reasons for the remarkable achievements in forest growth:

1.  *Increased Planting and Reforestation*:  Tree planting and reforestation efforts have been very extensive. Each year, approximately 2.6 million acres of trees are planted, an area roughly equal to the size of Connecticut.  The forest industry and private tree farmers together accounted for 87 percent of total tree plantings.

2.  *Fewer Losses due to Forest Fires*:  In the early 1900s, approximately 40 to 50 million acres were lost each year to fires.  Today, forest fire losses are approximately 4 million acres annually.

3.  *Increased Forestland Productivity*:  Forest productivity, the amount of wood grown per acre, has increased dramatically.  This has been due to improved management and care of our forests.  For example, in Indiana, a leader in hardwood productivity, the current average annual increase in growth per acre is about 140 board feet (12"x12"x1").  For example, "the average annual net volume growth of Indiana's forests has increased

substantially since 1967 and is now estimated to be 268.1 million cubic feet. The steepest increase in average annual net volume growth occurred since the last inventory in 1998."[1]

4.  *Engineering Improvements in Building Design*:  Engineering improvements in building designs have greatly lowered the amount of wood used per square foot of building space. Wood preservatives have also extended the service life of wood.

**OLD GROWTH FOREST:** The United States has 9.7 million acres of old growth forest. What constitutes an **old growth forest** varies from region to region, but generally it is a forest with a high percentage of very large trees at least 200 years old. About 8 million acres of such forests are protected within national parks, wilderness areas, and other set asides.  Most of the old growth forests are in the West, although some pockets exist in the eastern part of the country.  Where old growth forests are harvested, they are cut at a rate of about 1 percent a year and then are replanted.  Set-aside forests not used for commercial purposes will some day become old growth forests.

# Managing Our Forests

Healthy, productive forests don't just happen.  They require years of careful management and protection.  In the past, forestlands in the United States were not managed carefully, and in many areas were badly abused and neglected.  Although forest management is much better today, there is always a need for better conservation practices and management by all who own or use our forests

**PRINCIPLES OF FOREST MANAGEMENT:** A basic principle of forest management is **scientific conservation, i.e., "wise use"**.  This involves using forest resources for social and economic benefits without destroying the use of the resources for future generations.  This principle differs from **forest preservation**, the restricting of any commercial activity so forests can be passed on to future generations in a natural state.  Most public forestlands are managed according to scientific conservation, the exceptions being the set-aside preservation areas.  By federal law, the principles of multiple use and sustained yield must complement the principle of scientific conservation on public forestlands.  **Multiple-use management** requires the simultaneous use of forests for timber harvesting, recreation, watershed protection, cattle/sheep grazing, and wildlife habitat.  **Sustained yield management** means that forests must provide a continuous high level of forest product output without impairing future forestland productivity. The concept of sustained yield is similar to that of a bank account, where the interest earned is analogous to the growth of forest.  To ensure a sustained yield, a timber land owner would harvest only the tree growth that equates to living off the interest of a bank account and never letting the account go below the original amount of the principal.

**FOREST MANAGEMENT VERSUS ENVIRONMENTAL CONCERNS:** The forest management principles of scientific management, multiple use, and sustained yield can be interpreted in various ways and sometimes seem to work against each other.  An example is the Northern Spotted Owl controversy in the Pacific Northwest. Environmentalists claimed that old

1.  Christopher Woodall et al. *Indiana's Forests 1999-2003. Part A*. USDA Forest Service, Forest Inventory and Analysis Program, St. Paul, MN, page 22.

growth timber harvests endanger the owl's habitat.  Timber companies argued that limited harvesting will not endanger the species, but will greatly harm families whose livelihoods depend on timber harvesting.

Despite the controversies and conflicts that take place, the principles of scientific management, multiple use, and sustained yield are considered by many to be reasonable guidelines for the practical management of public and private lands.  As one author put it, "Most controversies are not over the principles themselves, but how they are applied."[2]

**IMPROVING FOREST MANAGEMENT:**  The application of wise conservation practices and management by both private and public forest owners has resulted in great improvements in the productivity of our nation's forests during the past 80 years.  There has been a growing awareness of the need to manage our complex forest ecosystems more carefully and not to view them solely as a source of timber.  More care than ever is being given to preserving wildlife habitat, watersheds, and recreation areas.  With proper management, these nontimber uses of our forestland can flourish, even on forestlands used primarily for timber.

There are many resources available for improving forest anagement.  The United States Department of Agriculture and various state government agencies offer consulting services, print information, and many other forest improvement programs.  Large forest companies also provide excellent resources in forest management.  Another valuable resource is the American Tree Farm System.  Established in 1941, the Tree Farm System is an organization of private forestland owners whose lands meet certain forest management criteria.  The farms are inspected every five years by volunteer foresters to ensure that the forests continue to be well tended.  Today there are over 73,000 tree farms, totaling over 29 million acres.

# Summary

The days have ended when forests can be viewed only as a source of timber.  Forest management must take into consideration all of the benefits our forests provide.  The good news is that responsible management of our forests can enable us to enjoy all of the many benefits that forests provide — now and into the future.  As the U.S. Forest Service states:

When a forest is managed properly, it can provide diversified value with a variety of habitat for wildlife, numerous recreational opportunities, scenic landscapes, jobs which help support a rural lifestyle, clean air, stable soil, high quality water, wood products which we need every day, and healthy trees for the future.[3]

---

2.  G. Tyler Miller, Jr. *Resource Conservation and Management.*  (Belmont, California, Wadsworth Publishing Company, 1990),  p. 391.

3.  Tomorrow's Forests Begin Today: The How and the Why of Good Forest Management, *U.S. Forest Service, U.S. Government Printing Office, 1988.*

# Teaching Activities

# Teaching Instructions

## Overview:

The specific teaching activities do not have to be done in order. However, you may want to do the Case Study toward the end of the unit after students have mastered much of the basic information. Some of the basic information to teach your students is found in the preceding *Facts About Forests and Forest Management* section. Other information is available from a variety of sources, many of which are listed in this booklet's *Resources* section. Encourage your students to research this information on their own. The Further Explorations Activity suggests a variety of research activities.

Some of the key economic concepts your students should learn in this unit on Trees and Forests are described immediately below in the "Key Concepts to Emphasize" section. These concepts are often highlighted in the "Key Questions to Ask Students" section of specific teaching activities.

## Key Concepts to Emphasize:

1. **Scarcity:** Trees, like all other productive resources are considered "scarce," since at a zero price there are not enough trees to satisfy all wants for them. This does *not* mean that forest resources are dwindling. In fact, our forests are producing more wood fiber than is being used.

2. **Forest Management Requires Scarce Productive Resources:** Productive, healthy forests require knowledgeable, skilled labor resources and adequate capital resources. Forest managers should understand the latest scientific management principles and have the proper equipment and technology to apply these principles. There is a cost to obtaining these scarce productive resources, as there is in any productive enterprise.

3. **Public Versus Private Ownership of Commercial Forests:** Most commercial timberland in the United States is privately owned (71 percent). Private individuals own 58 percent of this total. Most of the controversial issues that appear in the media involve forest management policies on *public* lands.

   Private forest owners and forest companies have an economic incentive to manage their forestlands intelligently since they will reap the benefits of good management. Poorly managed land tends to lose value, with the owner suffering the loss. A problem in some less developed countries is that individuals may have free access to commonly owned forestlands. This results in overuse since there is little economic incentive for individuals to manage commonly owned forests carefully. An example is the excess cutting of trees for firewood. Tree planting efforts by governments in less developed countries have had mixed results. The *World Development Report 1992*, published by the World Bank, reports that successful replanting efforts have taught an important lesson: "Trees can be a highly profitable commercial crop – but farmers must be given the right to own, cut, and sell them at fair market prices."[1]

---

1. World Bank, *World Development Report 1992* (New York: Oxford University Press, 1992), p. 141.

4. **Wood Prices, Profits, and Incentives:** The market price of wood is determined by its supply and demands and is a reflection of wood's relative scarcity. The market price for wood changes constantly, reflecting changes in supply and demand. In competitive markets, timber producers cannot set the price. They must accept the price that is determined by the market. Profit is the amount of money left over from sales revenues after all production costs have been paid. It can be expressed as an equation:

---

# PROFIT = SALES REVENUES — PRODUCTION COSTS

---

Tree farmers try to control their costs in order to increase profits. An increase in the market price also can increase profits. Of course, increasing costs and a decreasing market price will have the opposite effect.

An issue that has sparked some controversy is whether the market price of wood truly reflects the costs of production. Some environmentalists contend that wood producers do not bear the costs they impose on the environment, especially damage to wildlife habitat and loss of scenic beauty. They also contend that wood producers receive direct or indirect subsidies (artificially low harvesting fees, tax breaks, etc.) to harvest on public lands, which lowers timber production costs and artificially lowers the price of wood products. This low price then encourages people to purchase more wood products, putting more stress on our forests.

5. **Paper Recycling:** Students and the general public typically believe that recycling paper saves our forests from destruction. Actually, most trees used for paper production are planted on tree plantations and are harvested like other crops. As the demand for paper increases, farmers plant more trees. Also, much paper is made from wood residues created from the manufacture of wood products or from lower grade trees that have been thinned (culled) in order to improve the growth of the remaining trees. Paper recycling is a good way to reduce the amount going into landfills, but does not save our forests from destruction. Currently, the United States recycles about 42 percent of its paper.

6. **Assigning Monetary Values to Environmental Concerns:** One of the difficulties policymakers face is assigning monetary values when making decisions about the environment. For example, when considering whether to set aside additional wilderness areas, how does one put a price tag on the environmental value of scenic wilderness areas? On this particular issue, some believe that no price tag *can* be put on the value of wilderness. To them, setting aside wilderness is primarily a moral issue, not an economic one. This makes it very difficult for policymakers, who *must* consider economic costs and benefits in their decisions.

7. **Opportunity Costs and Trade-Offs:** Any public policy decision will involve opportunity costs and trade-offs among different policy goals. For example, setting aside more wilderness preservation areas means less wood harvested and, other things being equal, higher prices for wood products. Electing to set aside preservation areas means forgoing the commercial benefits of these areas. Wise public policy requires honest attempts to assess the true opportunity costs of policy options.

# Activity 1
## Leaves and Trees

---

**Teaching Objectives:** After completing this activity, students will be able to:

1.  Identify the leaves of various kinds of trees,

2.  Explain that some trees are more scarce than other trees,

3.  Explain that in the marketplace, trees that are relatively more scarce have a higher value and a higher market price.

**Time Allowed:** Three 30-minute periods

**Materials:**
- Leaves from the schoolyard, nearby park, or wooded area
- Drawing paper
- "Trees in Our Community" worksheet

## Vocabulary/Concepts:

- *Scarcity:* in economics, the condition of people not being able to have (at a zero price) all of the goods, services, or productive resources (including trees!) that they want. Because trees are scarce, people must make choices how to use them.

- *Price:* the amount people pay to buy a good, service, or productive resource. Differences in prices reflect differences in relative scarcity. Items which are relatively more scarce have a higher price than items that are relatively less scarce.

## Teaching Procedure:

1.  Put the word "tree" on the board. Ask students to tell all that they know about trees. Write the different student responses on the board. (concept map)

2.  Put one leaf on each student's desk. Have students write down the different characteristics of the leaf and read these characteristics to the class.

3.  Students then form "investigation teams" with other students who have the same type of leaf. The group chooses a recorder to record student observations and a group artist to draw the tree. Teams then go outside (schoolyard, park, or nearby wooded area) and find a tree that corresponds with the leaf. Each group must:

a. carefully observe the tree and identify characteristics that "make our tree special."

b. count how many of their particular tree there are in the schoolyard/park.

c. identify any benefits their particular tree provides.

d. identify any problems the tree might cause (growing too close to the building, in the way of a new soccer field, etc.).

4. Back in the classroom, discuss team observation. (Optional: Each student could write a paragraph about the group's observations.) Discuss the various benefits that trees provide in the schoolyard, park, or wooded area. Also, discuss the problems that certain trees can cause. Discuss whether there should be more or fewer trees in the schoolyard.

5. Distribute the "Trees in Our Community" worksheet. Explain how the bar graphs illustrate how many of each kind of tree were found.

6. Discuss where trees in schoolyards or parks come from. Have students call a local tree nursery and find out the **prices** of various trees they observed and the prices of other types of trees. List these prices on the board. Discuss why these prices vary. (Trees that are relatively more scarce have a higher value and price.)

## Teaching Tips:

1. Use words generated by the students for spelling, vocabulary, and writing stories.
2. Have students observe the trees in succeeding months, noting any changes.
3. Preserve leaves by pressing, dipping in wax, laminating, or covering with Elmer's glue.
4. Keep your own file of pressed, preserved leaves, or make a leaf "notebook."

## Key Questions to Ask Students:

1. Why don't we get more trees for the schoolyard? *(Trees are a scarce resource. They are not freely available. There are other important uses for the school's financial resources besides new trees.)*

2. When are trees not scarce in a schoolyard? *(When we sometimes need to get rid of them! The trees may be in the way of a new ball diamond, growing too near the building, etc.)*

3. Why do some trees cost more than others? *(Some trees have special characteristics that make them highly useful and highly valued.)*

## Bulletin Board Ideas:

1. Display the tree pictures and the corresponding observations of each team.
2. Press the leaves and make a "Bulletin Board Tree."
3. Display the prices of the trees found at local nurseries.
4. Make a "Trees are Special" bulletin board.
5. Cut out silhouettes of different tree species.

**Student Journal Ideas:**

1.  Draw a picture and make observations of a favorite tree.
2.  Write a paragraph about why "Trees are Special."
3.  Write a paragraph about why it was necessary to cut down a particular tree at home or in the neighborhood. What was the opportunity cost?
4.  Draw a picture of a particular tree in the schoolyard. Write a story from the *tree's* point of view, about what it's like to be a tree in the schoolyard.
5.  Write a paragraph about things that damage trees (pulling off bark, lawn mower, disease, salt, etc.).

# Trees in our Community

1. Make a bar graph showing how many of the different kinds of trees you found in your schoolyard, park, or wooded area. Use different colors in your graph and label it correctly. On the vertical axis, label the number of trees. On the horizontal axis, place the tree types.

2. Below are some of the benefits that trees provide for our cities and communities. Discuss these benefits with your class. Circle the <u>five</u> benefits that you think are the most important.

* produce oxygen
* provide privacy
* absorb carbon dioxide
* reduce soil erosion
* absorb and block noise

* provide color, flowers, and beautiful shapes
* trap dust and other pollutants
* shade and cool cities, reducing energy usage
* blocks winter winds, keeping buildings warm
* provide habitat and food for birds and animals

3.	In economics, **goods, services,** and **productive resources** (including trees) are considered **"scarce."** (This means that if they were <u>free,</u> there would not be enough for everyone to have all that they want.) The **price** of a good, service, or productive resource gives us a clue about how scarce it is compared to other things. For example, a car is relatively more scarce (more expensive!) than a bicycle; gold is more scarce than tin; and so on. Certain types of trees that are planted in communities have a higher price (are relatively more scarce) than other types because they have certain characteristics that make them more valuable to consumers.

In the blanks below, list five specific characteristics of certain trees that make them more valuable (and usually more expensive) to consumers than other trees.

a. _____

b. _____

c. _____

d. _____

e. _____

# Activity 2
## Our Valuable Trees – A Skit

---

**Teaching Objectives:** After completing this activity, students will be able to:

1. Identify characteristics of different trees.
2. Explain the economic concept of scarcity.

**Time Allowed:**     30 minutes

**Materials:**
- Skit cards
- "Tree" costumes (optional)

**Vocabulary/Concepts:**

- *Value:* the worth, importance, or usefulness of something.

- *Scarcity:* the condition of not being able to have (at a zero price) all of the goods, services, or productive resources (including trees!) that you want. Because trees are scarce, people must make choices about how to use them.

- *Price:* the amount people pay to buy a good, service, or productive resource. Differences in market prices reflect differences in relative scarcity. Items which are very valuable and scarce cost more than those which are not.

**Teaching Procedure:**

1. Give the skit cards to four students who want to present the brief skit to the class. Let these students plan and prepare the skit. (You may want to let groups of four students perform the skit to each other.)

2. After the skit, ask the class questions from the "Key Questions to Ask Students" section.

3. Let students ask their own questions based on information in the skit.

**Teaching Tips:**

1. Some students may want to make tree costumes.

2. You can divide the class into teams and have a "Jeopardy" type of contest using information from the skit.

## Key Questions to Ask Students:

1.  How are all these trees alike?  How are they different?  *(answers will vary)*

2.  In what ways are these trees valuable?  *(for wood products, habitat for animals, shade and beauty, etc.)*

3.  What are some of the scarce goods that come from each of these trees?  *(answers will vary)*

4.  What is the "clue" that lets consumers know how scarce a good or service is?  *(The price consumers pay is the key clue.  Items that are more valuable and relatively more scarce typically cost more.)*

5.  What are some specific characteristics of high quality wood that make it more scarce and valuable than low quality wood?  *(color, hardness, absence of knots, straightness, etc.)*

## Bulletin Board Ideas:

1.  Make Bulletin Board Trees using leaves representing the four different trees.  Label the trees with the appropriate characteristics.

## Student Journal Ideas:

1.  Research different trees and write a story about yourself as if you were the tree.

2.  Cut out pictures of homes that are well landscaped with trees and those that are not.  Write about the differences in the beauty and economic value of the homes.  Why are certain types of trees planted in certain places?  (Shade, wind break, etc.)

# SKIT CARD

## BLACK WALNUT TREE

I am one of America's most valuable trees.

At one time, even my stumps were sold!  My wood is rather scarce and costs a lot of money.

My wood is hard, heavy and has a beautiful dark brown color.  It is used for expensive furniture and fine items because it can have a glossy polish.

I may grow to be 80 feet tall in the woods.

I have dark brown, rough bark and beautiful, long compound leaves.

My leaves have a strong smell if you crush them in your hand.

My nuts fall in the autumn.  The squirrels like them, as do people.

The juice will stain your hands.  Squirrels that eat through the husk end up with a stained mouth!

What tree am I?

## ASPEN TREE

In our family, there are three of us:  the LARGETOOTH ASPEN, the QUAKING ASPEN, and the BALSAM POPLAR.

The largetooth and quaking aspen grow on uplands, even on sandy land.

We take very good care of the land because we grow quickly over land that has been burned.

We hold the soil so it does not erode when it rains.

We can grow new trees from our roots so a fire cannot kill us.

Our seeds have long hair-like threads which the wind can carry over a long distance.

We do not live very long, but remember, we grow fast.

The largetooth aspen has larger teeth on the leaves.

The quaking aspen leaves flutter in the breeze and make a soft rustling sound.

The quaking aspen is found over a larger area of North America than any other tree.

Because our wood is not as valuable and scarce as other woods, it is used for paper pulp, boxes, crates, and packing materials.

Our wood is very light and decays easily when put in the soil, which helps when it is discarded or put in landfills.

The balsam poplar likes to live by swamps and in moist soil of all kinds.

I can grow to 75 feet tall.

My trunk is straight and sometimes is three feet in diameter.

My wood is used for floors in barns and stables.

What tree am I?

# SUGAR MAPLE TREE

Although I grow very slowly, I have a straight trunk that can reach 50 feet or more.

My sap carries a lot of sugar in the spring.

I am asked to share some sap every year so that people can have syrup on their food and sugar to eat.

People bore holes into my trunk and put little spouts in the holes. My sap drips into a bucket hung on the spout. This sap is boiled to make syrup and boiled more to make sugar.

I can share my sap every year if people are careful.

My wood is also very valuable. It is used for hardwood floors, furniture, and baskets.

My wood makes excellent firewood, too.

I grow in parks and upland woods. I can even grow in the shade under other trees.

I don't like the ground to be too wet or too dry.

Animals live in my branches, and I help reduce soil erosion.

I am a wonderful shade tree, and I make people's homes much more beautiful and valuable.

All in all, I am one of the finest trees!

What tree am I?

# TULIP TREE

I am the state tree of Indiana.

I grow very tall and straight.

Some of us have even grown as high as 200 feet and are 8-10 feet in diameter!

My buds are reddish-blue and look like a beaver's tail until they open.

My flower is very showy and looks like a magnolia.

I am found in upland woods, large parks, and moist woodlands.

My leaves are shiny green and turn yellow in the autumn. They look like a tulip from the side. No other leaf is like mine.

My wood is valuable. It is used for woodwork inside homes, furniture, shingles, and boats.

I provide a home for animals and help reduce soil erosion.

I am a wonderful shade tree, and I help make people's homes more beautiful and valuable.

Although most of us were cut when settlers first came, we have come back to become one of the most abundant trees in Indiana.

I am proud to be the state tree of Indiana.

What tree am I?

# Activity 3
## Forests and Forest Products

---

**Teaching Objectives:** After completing this activity, students will be able to:

1.  Identify a variety of forest products.
2.  Explain that there are many competing uses for wood.
3.  Identify the opportunity cost of particular choices involving wood use.

**Time Allowed:** 30 – 45 minutes

**Materials:**
- Class list for each student
- "What We Get From Trees"
- "Our Valuable Forest Products" worksheet

## Vocabulary/Concepts:

- *Forest Products:* the large variety of goods produced from forests, including lumber, plywood, furniture, nuts, syrup, adhesives, mulches, inks, fertilizers, etc.

- *Opportunity Cost:* the single most valuable alternative given up when a choice is made. Every producer and consumer economic decision has an opportunity cost.

- *Productive Resources:* the inputs (natural, human, and capital) needed to produce goods and services.

## Teaching Procedure:

1.  Write the word "forest" on the board. Ask students to identify what they think of when they think of forests. Record student responses using a concept map.

2.  Circle the responses on the concept map that name **forest products** (lumber, furniture, syrup, nuts, logs, paper, etc.). Discuss how these products benefit our homes and communities.

3.  Pass out a class list with blank lines next to each name. Ask students to write the name of a forest product beside their name.

4.  Give students about 15 minutes to move quietly around the classroom and get each classmate to write a product next to his or her name. The name of a product may only be used once. If the paper a student is signing already has his or her product on it, the student must write another product.

5. The students now have a list of forest products. How many more can they identify that have not been mentioned? This list can be put on a chart or on the board (Use the "What We Get From Trees" handout for additional examples of forest products.)

6. Identify a forest product, such as furniture. Discuss all the **productive resources** that are needed to make the product. (**Human resources** such as lumbermen and foresters, and **capital resources,** such as chainsaws, factory equipment, etc.)

7. Review the concept of **opportunity cost**. Discuss the opportunity cost of using some wood to produce a piece of furniture (the next best use of that wood, i.e. what the wood *would* have been used for if it had not been used for furniture.)

8. Have students complete the "Our Valuable Forest Products" worksheet.

## Teaching Tips:

1. Save the Concept Map and Student Product Lists to use in the next activity.

## Key Questions to Ask Students:

1. How are forest products valuable and beneficial to you and your community? *(They make our lives easier and more enjoyable, provide jobs and income for people, etc.)*

2. What kind of productive resource is wood? *(a natural resource)*

3. Why are all forest products "scarce?" *(They are not freely available at a zero price. They all command a price in the marketplace.)*

4. What is the opportunity cost of using a tree for lumber? *(the next best alternative use)*

5. What are some of the other uses for our forests besides forest products? *(habitat for animals, recreation, source of oxygen, watershed protection, scenic beauty, etc.)*

## Bulletin Board Ideas:

1. Label pictures of common and unique forest products or create a display of real products.
2. Display student poems or essays about trees and forests.

## Student Journal Ideas:

1. Write a paragraph on "How forests are important to me."
2. Identify forest products used in my home.
3. Draw a picture of a furniture producer having to decide to use a particular piece of wood to make a table **or** a cabinet. Show the opportunity cost of the decision. Write a short description of the picture.
4. Draw certain forest products. List the productive resources needed to produce these products.

# Our Valuable Forest Products

1.  In the space below, draw a picture of a forest product.  Below the product, list some of the **productive resources** needed to produce it.

| **Natural Resources** | **Human Resources** | **Capital Resources** |
|---|---|---|
| _____ | _____ | _____ |
| _____ | _____ | _____ |

2.  Below are pictures of two **forest products.**

    a.  Which of these is **scarce?**       the table      the pencil    the pencil and the table

    b.  Which of these is **more** scarce?    the pencil    the table

    c.  How do you know which is relatively more scarce? _____
    _____

3.  Our forests have many other valuable uses besides forest products.  In the blanks below, list at least four other uses of our forests.

    1. _____        3. _____

    2. _____        4. _____

4.  A tree farmer decided to use one of his trees for firewood instead of selling it for lumber.  What was his **opportunity cost** of using the tree for firewood?
    _____

# What We Get From Trees

Nuts and fruits

| | |
|---|---|
| Foliage | oils, extract, decorations |
| Sap | syrup blend, sugar, syrup |
| Bark | drugs, dye, oils, tannin, mulches |
| Stumps | veneer, distillates: charcoal, pine oil, pitch, tar oil, wood resin, wood tar, wood turpentine |
| Roots | smoking pipes, tea, oil |
| Gums | storax: adhesives, chewing gum, flavoring extracts, ointments, perfumes |
| Hapten | solvent, standard for octane rating |
| Balsam | drugs, glass cement, spirit varnishes |
| Spruce | chewing gum, confections, drugs |
| Resins | gum turpentine: cleaning fluids, crayons, explosives, floor polish, greases and oils, insecticides, paints, stains, varnishes, shoe polish, soaps, synthetic camphor, waxes wood filters |
| | gum resin: ceramic enamels, disinfectants, drugs, electrical insulation, fireworks and explosives, greases, leather dressings, paint driers, printing ink, soaps, solder flux, waxes |
| Charcoal Distillates | oils, acetate of line, acetic acid, charcoal, tar, wood alcohol, wood creosote |
| Lignin | plastics, road building materials, soil conditioner, tanning materials |
| Cellulose | fiber products: paper, pulp, and paper products, fiberboard, and other examples too obvious and too long to list |
| Chemical Products | artificial hair and bristles, cellophane, celluloid, collodion, explosives, imitation leather, molded plastics, phonograph records, photo films, rayon, sausage cases, shatterproof glass, solid alcohol, sponges |
| Logs | lumber, residues, ties, veneer, posts, poles, piling, and other examples too obvious and too long to list |

# Activity 4
## Forest Benefits and Conflicting Goals

---

**Teaching Objectives:** After completing this activity, students will be able to:

1.    Identify different benefits of our forests.
2.    Identify conflicts that arise in managing forests.
3.    Identify opportunity costs and trade-offs in forest management.

**Time Allowed:**    30 minutes

**Materials:**    • Chalkboard or Overhead Projector

**Vocabulary/Concepts:**

- *Forest Conservation:* using forests for social and economic benefits, without destroying their use for future generations.

- *Forest Preservation:* restricting any commercial activity in a forest so that forests can be passed on to future generations in a natural state.

- *Watershed:* any given area of land which drains or sheds water to the same point.

- *Multiple-use:* using forests for more than one thing at a time. Recreation and wildlife are two uses that can often work well together.

- *Habitat:* the native environment of a plant or animal.

- *National Forests:* "working forests" established by the federal government to ensure a continual supply of wood.

- *Opportunity Cost:* the value of one's next best alternative when making a decision. Every producer and consumer economic decision has an opportunity cost.

- *Trade-Off:* giving up some of one thing in order to get some of another.

**Teaching Procedure:**

1.    Write the word "forests" on the board or overhead. Ask students to identify specific benefits of our forests. Record these in the form of a concept map.

2.    Write the following general categories of forest benefits/goals on the board: **Forest Products, Recreation, Wildlife Habitat, Watershed Protection,** and **Source of Oxygen.** Have individual students come to the board and categorize a specific benefit under these general categories. Continue until all words are categorized.

3. Explain how some of these forest benefits can result in conflicts about how to use and manage forests. For example, how could obtaining forest products conflict with protecting wildlife habitat or using forests for recreation?

4. Conduct a class "debate," letting students role-play representatives from interested parties (lumber company owner, nature park guide, hunter, etc.) who want to have a say in how a certain piece of forestland should be managed.

5. Explain how careful forest management helps minimize the conflict among various forest benefits/goals. (Review pages 57-64)

6. Have students write a paragraph on what they would do to manage their own tree farm to minimize the conflict among the general forest benefits/goals.

## Key Questions to Ask Students:

1. Suppose Mr. Jones decides to use his forestland to open a campground instead of using it for lumber. What is his opportunity cost? *(giving up the benefits of using the forest for lumber.)* What is his opportunity cost if he decides to use the forestland for lumber? *(giving up the benefits of using the forestland as a campground.)*

2. Mrs. Smith decides not to cut down and sell all the trees on her tree farm so that the animals will have a place to live. What trade-off is she making? *(She is trading off the monetary benefits of cutting more wood for better protection of wildlife habitat.)*

3. Why do we have to make choices about how to use our forests? *(Forestland, like other natural resources, is a scarce resource. There are not enough forests to satisfy all of our wants; thus, we have to choose how to use them.)*

4. In what ways can cutting down some trees in a forest help the forest grow and help in other ways? *(Selective harvests help the remaining trees become more healthy and vigorous, thereby producing more oxygen; forests with some clear openings generally produce better wildlife habitat; logging roads used to access harvested trees can later help recreationists gain access to parts of the forest that otherwise would not be accessible.)*

5. At Oakdale School, six large oak trees are in the way of a new softball/kickball field the students want. Should the trees be removed? What are the opportunity costs and the trade-offs?

## Bulletin Board Ideas:

1. Display five different forest benefits/goals. Cut out and categorize pictures under them.

## Student Journal Ideas:

1. List and define the vocabulary words in this activity.
2. Explain the difference between forest *conservation* and forest *preservation.*

# Activity 5
## Forest Economics

**Teaching Objectives:** After completing this activity, students will be able to:

1. Identify the three basic productive resources.
2. Identify productive resources necessary to manage a tree farm.
3. Predict changes in the market price of wood given changes in supply and demand.

**Time Allowed:** 30 minutes

**Materials:**
- "Forest Economics" worksheet

**Vocabulary/Concepts:**

- *Productive Resources:* the inputs (natural, human, and capital) needed to produce goods and services

- *Market Price:* price of a good, service, or productive resource as determined by its supply and demand in the marketplace. If other things do not change, an increase in supply or a decrease in demand will cause the market price to fall; a decrease in supply or an increase in demand will cause the market price to rise.

**Teaching Procedure:**

1. Explain/discuss **productive resources.** Ask students to identify the productive resources needed to produce a chair or table. Write these on the board.

2. Discuss **market price.** Explain that the market price is a reflection of how **scarce** a good or service is compared to other goods and services. Goods and services that are relatively more scarce have higher prices than those that are less scarce.

3. Explain how changes in **supply** and **demand** cause changes in the prices of goods or services.

4. Have students complete the Forest Economics worksheet. Discuss answers.

**Teaching Tips:**

1. Some students may want to know what causes changes in supply and demand. The primary factor that influences supply is a change in production costs. Factors that change demand are changes in income, prices of substitutes or complements, population size, or consumer tastes.

**Student Journal Ideas:**

1. Write a paragraph entitled, "Why Prices Change."

# Forest Economics

1.  Suppose you own a tree farm. You want to make money from your
    farm by selling timber, but you also want to protect wildlife habitats,
    the watershed, and recreational activities, such as hunting, camping, and fishing.
    List some of the **productive resources** you would need to manage your tree farm
    effectively.

    **Natural Resources**         **Human Resources**         **Capital Resources**

    _____              _____              _____

    _____              _____              _____

    _____              _____              _____

2.  Describe some things you could do to make sure that your timber harvesting does
    not hurt wildlife, cause soil erosion, or ruin recreation activities?

    _____

    _____

    _____

    _____

3.  In the following situations, will the **market price** for wood *increase* or *decrease?*
    Circle the correct response.

    a.  The wood supply does not change, but wood demand increases.

        The market price will:          increase          or          decrease

    b.  The wood demand does not change, but wood supply increases.

        The market price will:          increase          or          decrease

    c.  The wood supply does not change, but the wood demand decreases.

        The market price will:          increase          or          decrease

    d.  The wood demand does not change, but the wood supply decreases.

        The market price will:          increase          or          decrease

4.  Discuss with your teacher what could cause changes in supply and demand.

# Activity 6
## Conducting a Forest Survey

---

**Teaching Objective:** After completing this activity, students will be able to:

1. Conduct a survey to gather data about forests.
2. Tabulate, graph, and interpret data collected from a survey.

**Time Allowed:**     One 45-minute period plus out of class work

**Materials:**
- 10 survey forms for each student
- One "Forest Survey Final Data Sheet" for each student

## Teaching Procedure:

1. Each student interviews 10 different people using the survey form. (Interview *two* people from *each* age group.) Compile the data on a "Final Data Sheet," showing how those from each age group responded to the questions. <u>Note</u>: Some correct survey responses are: 2a. and 2b. Private individuals  3. Federal  4. Increasing  8. United States  9. 42 percent.

2. Students then write a paragraph explaining whether they agree or disagree with the general opinions of the survey respondents.

3. Compile the data from the entire class. Put this data in various graphic forms. Analyze and discuss the data, answering these types of questions:

   a. Did responses vary depending on the age of the respondent?
   b. On which question did respondents agree most? Least?
   c. Do you feel that this survey gave an accurate view about how people feel about forests? Why or why not?
   d. What could be done to make any survey more accurate? (*Interview more people.*)
      What are the trade-offs of interviewing more people? (*More accurate, but more costly, especially in terms of time!*)
   e. In general, how knowledgeable were respondents on the subject of forests?
   f. How could this level of knowledge be improved?
   g. Would responses vary if respondents worked in the forest products industry?

4. Have students write a report describing the entire survey project.

## Bulletin Board Ideas:

1. Create a bulletin board entitled, "Our Survey Results." Display the graphs and charts generated from the survey data.

# Forest Survey Form

Person Number # _____  Male _____  Female _____

Occupation _____

Age (circle one)    7-12        13-30        21-35      36-50      Over 50

| | | | | |
|---|---|---|---|---|
| 1. | How important are our forest resources to our country | Very Important | Somewhat Important | Not Very Important |
| 2a. | Commercial timberland is forestland that is available for growing and harvesting trees. In the United States, who owns most of this land? | Government | Forest Industry | Private Individuals |
| 2b. | In Indiana, who owns most of this land? | Government | Forest Industry | Private Individuals |
| 3. | Which level of government plays the largest role in managing public forestlands? | Federal | State | Local |
| 4. | Are forest and timber resources in the United States declining, staying about the same, or increasing? | Declining | Staying About the Same | Increasing |
| 5. | "Wilderness" is land set aside for noncommercial use, where there are no roads, permanent buildings, etc. Should the United States set aside more wilderness areas? | Yes | Maybe | No |
| 6. | Should the United States set aside more wilderness areas if it means higher prices for wood products and other natural resources and the loss of jobs for some timber workers? | Yes | Maybe | No |
| 7. | Can forestland that is used for timber harvesting still offer adequate protection for wildlife habitats? | Yes | Maybe | No |
| 8. | The world's largest producer of forest products is: | United States  Russia | | Canada |
| 9. | The United States currently recycles about what percentage of its paper? | 5%        15% | 35% | 42% |

# Forest Survey Final Data Sheet

| Survey Question | Respondent Age | | | | |
|---|---|---|---|---|---|
| | 7-12 | 13-20 | 21-35 | 36-50 | Over 50 |
| 1. Very Important | | | | | |
| Somewhat Important | | | | | |
| Not Very Important | | | | | |
| 2a. Government | | | | | |
| Forest Industry | | | | | |
| Private Individuals | | | | | |
| 2b. Government | | | | | |
| Forest Industry | | | | | |
| Private Individuals | | | | | |
| 3. Federal | | | | | |
| State | | | | | |
| Local | | | | | |
| 4. Declining | | | | | |
| Staying Same | | | | | |
| Increasing | | | | | |
| 5. Yes | | | | | |
| Maybe | | | | | |
| No | | | | | |
| 6. Yes | | | | | |
| Maybe | | | | | |
| No | | | | | |
| 7. Yes | | | | | |
| Maybe | | | | | |
| No | | | | | |
| 8. United States | | | | | |
| Russia | | | | | |
| Canada | | | | | |
| 9. 5% | | | | | |
| 15% | | | | | |
| 33% | | | | | |
| 42% | | | | | |

# Activity 7
## Making Recycled Paper

**Teaching Objectives:** After completing this activity, students will be able to:

1. Make recycled paper.
2. Identify reasons for recycling paper.
3. Identify resources that are conserved by recycling.
4. Identify the costs associated with recycling.

**Time Allowed:** 40-60 minutes

**Materials:** Each group of five or six students will need:

- bucket or large bowl
- newspaper
- rolling pin
- dry or liquid starch
- egg beater, hand mixer, or blender
- non rusting window screen
- flat pan a little larger than the screen
- hot water

## Vocabulary/Concepts:

- *Softwood:* wood from conifer (cone-bearing) trees, called evergreens

- *Wood fiber:* a threadlike part of the tissue of a tree

- *Recycle:* to use again in the same or different way

## Teaching Procedure:

1. Tear the newspaper into very small pieces and put in the bowl. Pour in hot water (2 cups of water to 1/2 cup of shredded paper). Let soak for a few minutes.

2. Beat the paper and water to make pulp until the mixture is the consistency of cooked oatmeal. Add one tablespoon of dry or liquid starch and mix well. The starch helps hold the paper together.

3. Pour the mixture into the flat pan. Slide the screen into the bottom of the pan and allow the pulp to settle onto it.

4. Lift the screen out carefully. Let drain for a minute. Place the screen between some newspaper. Squeeze out the rest of the water using the rolling pin. Repeat if necessary.

5. Remove the screen and allow to dry. Peel the new paper off the screen. It will probably look more like gray cardboard, but it is recycled paper.

## Teaching Tips:

1. Try letting different groups use different types of paper, including notebook paper, slick paper, cardboard, and construction paper.

2. You can use an embroidery hoop to hold the screen.

3. To make white paper, add detergent. To make colored paper, add food coloring or scraps of construction paper.

4. Use magnifying lens and/or a microscope to compare the fibers of the recycled paper and other kinds of paper.

## Key Questions to Ask Students:

1. What productive resources did we use to make the recycled paper? (*natural resources/ raw materials – water, old paper, starch; human resources – ourselves; capital resources – bucket, rolling pin, egg beater, screen, pan*)

2. Why are these resources considered "scarce?" (*They are not freely available in unlimited quantities.*)

3. Do we save trees when we recycle? (*Fewer trees have to be cut down if we recycle. However, much wood pulp is waste from wood product manufacturing, and the trees used for paper are typically grown on tree farms and are harvested like any other crop. There is not a static, fixed supply of wood. If consumers want more paper products and the demand for paper, therefore, increases, then tree farmers will likely grow more trees. Perhaps the greatest advantage of recycling paper is the reduced amount going into landfills. This means less spent on expensive tipping fees.*)

4. Why don't we recycle all types of paper, such as paper napkins or tissue paper? (*The benefits of doing so would be too small relative to the expense of collecting and processing these types. Also, paper towels, napkins, and tissue paper are not recycled because of harmful bacteria.*)

## Bulletin Board Ideas:

1. Display the handmade paper on a bulletin board that encourages students to recycle waste paper from their school.
2. Press the damp paper over forms made by students and display the resulting "sculptures."

## Student Journal Ideas:

1. Write a paragraph on the paper you've just recycled describing how you made your recycled paper.

# Activity 8
## Further Explorations

1. Research job specialization in forest management, such as botanist, ecologist, forester, land use planner, naturalist, park administrator, recreation specialist, timber manager, wildlife biologist. Find out such things as: What education/training is required? How many job openings are there? How much is the pay? What are the other benefits?

2. Visit a tree farm and nature preserve. Observe and note the different types of management practices and prepare a report for your class.

3. Design a conservation area on your school grounds. Investigate the types of trees that would grow best and the type of care they would need. Research the economic value of the trees. Could the trees be sold to provide funds for the school in later years? What other benefits might the school get from the trees? Who would care for this area when your class graduates?

4. Identify forests on a state map. Color code the forests to identify which are owned by the government and which are privately owned. Who owns the most acreage?

5. Visit a paper recycling plant. Find out how you can save paper and where it goes when you recycle it. Does your school buy recycled paper? Does your school recycle it? What kind of paper can be recycled at the plant? What economic problems with supply and demand does the recycling plant face? What productive resources are saved by recycling paper?

6. Investigate a paper manufacturer. What products do they produce? Is their product made wholly or partially from recycled paper? Does cost enter into this decision? How many times can wood fiber be recycled?

7. Write a report about buying a cut tree for Christmas or purchasing a balled tree that can be planted later. What are some of the reasons many people purchase an artificial tree? What happens to the old artificial tree when the family decides to get a different artificial tree?

8. Indiana is known for hardwood trees. What are some different kinds of hardwood trees, and how are they used? How old are the trees when they are cut? Why? How do hardwood trees benefit the Indiana economy?

9. Research the ways that trees add value to private residences. Ask a local real estate agent or nursery owner for information.

10. Identify wildlife that live in the woods, tree farm, or nature preserves nearest your home. Where does the wildlife live? What do they eat? Are any considered a nuisance?

11.    Research the spotted owl controversy in the Pacific Northwest. What were the "trade-offs" involved in this controversy?

12.    Compare and contrast National Forests, National Parks, Wilderness Areas, Nature Preserves, and Tree Farms.

13.    Research which types of trees are the most valuable for furniture. Why?

14.    Find magazine or newspaper articles about trees. Do you agree or disagree with the position of the author?

15.    We have had many forest fires. Are there reasons to let the forests burn? Why or why not? What would you do if you were the manager of a forest that caught fire from a careless camper?

16.    New technologies, such as wood gasification, are now available for using wood to heat homes and schools very efficiently. Investigate these new technologies. Should they be used more?

17.    New, fast growing "super trees" are being developed. Investigate these new trees. What promise do they hold for the future?

18.    Research different tree-harvesting methods, including clear-cutting, seed tree selection, and selective cutting.

19.    Investigate how trees help conserve energy in urban areas.

20.    Research how much it costs timber companies to harvest trees on public lands. Do companies receive subsidies from the government, or do harvesting fees reflect the true benefits of being allowed to harvest trees?

21.    Research the serious problem of the Emerald Ash Borer. How is the danger of these insects being handled?

# Activity 9
## Let's Talk it Over

**Teaching Suggestions:** Discuss the challenging (and sometimes controversial!) statements and questions below with your students. Help the students think critically by applying the concepts learned in this unit. Be prepared for some lively discussion.

1. In the Pacific Northwest, the federal government did not let logging companies cut as much wood as before. The reason was to protect the habitat of the spotted owl. As a result of this policy, many loggers lost their jobs and had difficulty getting new jobs. Their families are suffering. Do you agree with the government policy? What would <u>you</u> do?

2. Clear-cutting means cutting all the trees from an area and then replanting them all at once. What are the advantages and disadvantages of clear-cutting? Should clear-cutting be allowed? Why or why not?

3. "Recycling saves our forests from destruction." Do you agree or disagree with this statement? Explain.

4. Do you think the government should require all people and businesses to recycle paper, no matter where they live? Discuss this with your classmates.

5. "Cutting down some trees in a forest can be helpful for the other trees." True or False? Explain your answer.

6. To help the United States import less oil from other countries, do you think the government should encourage people to use wood to heat their homes?

7. "The government should set aside more wilderness preservation areas, where no commercial activity is allowed, even if this means higher prices for wood products." Do you agree or disagree? Explain.

8. If there is any risk at all that an animal species could be harmed by timber harvesting, do you think the harvesting should be stopped? Why or why not? Defend your position.

9. "To promote the use of renewable resources, schools should investigate other heating choices, such as burning wood." Do you agree or disagree? Explain.

10. "There should be no timber cutting at all in our national forests." Do you agree or disagree? Explain your position.

11. "Local taxes should be increased to pay for tree plantings in cities and communities." Agree or disagree?

# Activity 10
## EEE Actions: You Can Make A Difference!

1. Plant at least one tree at your home or in your community.

2. Recycle all your newspapers and junk mail.

3. Reuse items as much as possible. For example, use old newspapers for painting or pet cages and use junk mail envelopes for storing photographs or notes.

4. When practical, write on both sides of the paper.

5. Invite a relative or friend who is knowledgeable about trees or forests to visit your classroom and share his or her expertise.

6. Visit a forest, tree farm, or nature preserve with your family.

7. Take a younger child by the hand and help him or her enjoy the trees as much as you do.

8. Consider paying a little more for recycled paper. Help "close the circle" on recycled paper.

9. Don't plant large trees near electric lines. Plant trees elsewhere or plant dwarf trees instead.

10. List ways that you can inform friends, relatives, and others in the community about what you learned about forests. Put some of these plans into action.

11. What have you learned about trees and forests that surprised you during this study? Will you change your habits or beliefs because of what you have learned? Will you try to persuade others to believe the way you do?

# Activity 11
## The Case of the Class Field Trip

**Teaching Objectives:** After completing this activity, students will be able to:

1. Analyze a problem using a decision model.
2. Understand that decisions involve trade-offs among competing goals.

**Time Allowed:** 30 minutes

**Materials:**
- Scenario – the Case of the Class Field Trip
- Decision Tree or Decision Grid Handouts pages 20-22

## Vocabulary/Concepts:

- *Opportunity Cost:* the value of one's next best alternative when making a decision.

- *Trade-offs:* giving up some of one thing in order to get some of another

## Teaching Procedure:

1. Divide the class into groups or work together as a large group. Pass out "The Case of the Class Field Trip."

2. Use the Decision Tree or Five Step Model to solve the case study. Have students present and discuss their decisions.

3. Discuss student responses to the questions below the case study.

# Case Study

## Case of the Class Field Trip

**Student Directions:**

1.  Read the case study below and determine what decision the class should make. Use the Decision Tree to help you decide.

2.  After you have made a decision, answer the questions below.

---

### Scenario

Washington School 4th graders have been studying about trees and forests all year. The class is now very excited because it has just received a special invitation from the Forest Service to visit a beautiful national forest located 50 miles away. Foresters will camp overnight with the class and will do many fun activities to teach the students more about trees and forests. There will also be time for swimming, hiking, and sports activities. The two-day field trip, including all meals, will cost the whole class only $600. Quite a deal!

However, the camping trip has created a difficult problem. The class had been planning to help build an outdoor laboratory for the school, complete with pond, bushes, and a forested area. One of the student's parents, a landscape planner, has just found out that he can get 20 good sized trees for the new outdoor laboratory for only $600.

The class has saved $600 by doing various business projects and fund raisers. How should the class spend the money? Should they go on the trip and enjoy learning about the forests or should they spend the money on trees for the outdoor lab that people will enjoy for years?

---

## Questions:

1.  What is the scarcity problem in this case study? _____
    _____

2.  What is the opportunity cost of your decision? _____
    _____

3.  Does every decision have an opportunity cost? _____ Explain _____
    _____
    _____

4.  What were the trade-offs in this case study? _____
    _____
    _____

# Answers to Selected Questions in Teaching Activities

**Activity 1 - Trees in Our Community:** 2. Answers will vary. 3. disease resistant, fruit bearing, specific size or shape, fast-growing, special fall color, attractive berries, attractive patterns in wood, etc.

**Activity 3 - Our Valuable Forest Products:** 1. Answers will vary. 2a. both the pencil and the table. 2b. the table 2c. It has a higher price. 3. source of oxygen, wildlife habitat, recreation, watershed protection. 4. The opportunity cost is giving up the benefits of selling it as lumber.

**Activity 5 - Forest Economies:** 1. Natural: water, sun, soil, fertilizer, etc. Human: biologist, forest manager, wildlife specialist, lumberman, trucker, etc. Capital: chainsaws, trucks, chains, ax, bird feeders, campfire grills, etc. 2. leave trees and shrubs standing for wildlife, avoid excessive cutting to guard against erosion, build special areas for camping and hiking, etc. 3a. increase 3b. decrease 3c. decrease 3d. increase

**Activity 11 - Case Study:** Students will have differing opinions on which is the best choice. It depends on the weight they attach to the criteria.

**Decision Tree Model:** *Choice 1* – Go on Trip; <u>Good Points:</u> fun activities, not expensive, will learn about forests. <u>Bad Points:</u> Only lasts two days, doesn't help school. *Choice 2* – Lab: <u>Good Points:</u> helps school, good price on trees. <u>Bad Points:</u> not as much fun

| Decision-Making Grid Answer Key<br>The Case of the Class Field Trip | | | | |
|---|---|---|---|---|
| **Criteria** | | | | |
| **Alternatives** | **Fun** | **Helps School** | **Long Run Effect** | **Learn About Forests** |
| **Go on Trip** | + | - | - | + |
| **Trees for Lab** | - | + | + | - |

**Questions:** 1. The scarcity problem is, given budget constraints, the class cannot do both the field trip and the tree planting. 2. The opportunity cost of the field trip was giving up the tree purchase; the opportunity cost of the tree purchase was giving up the field trip.

# Unit 3

# Water Resources

# Overview of Unit 3

## Water Resources

**Introduction:**

In this unit, students explore the value of our water resources. Students learn how water resources can become polluted and they investigate the costs involved in cleanup. Students also learn that it is impractical to have perfectly clean water, and that to some extent, all water is "polluted." Students discover that the cost of getting our water cleaner and cleaner eventually becomes prohibitive. At that point, it is better to use our scarce productive resources for some other valuable purpose.

**Learning Objectives:**

After completing this unit, students will be able to:

1. Understand basic facts about water resources.
2. Identify ways that water resources become polluted.
3. Identify some of the costs involved in cleaning up water resources.
4. Explain why insisting on zero pollution is not wise public policy.

**Unit Outline:**

I. Facts About Water Resources

II. Teaching Instructions and Key Concepts To Emphasize

III. Specific Teaching Activities

1. The Water Cycle: Along for the Ride!
2. Can Water Be Hard?
3. Does Clean Mean Pristine?
4. Decision Time in Bonedry, California
5. Is Cleaning Hazardous To Your Health?
6. Further Explorations
7. Let's Talk It Over
8. EEE Actions — You Can Make a Difference!
9. Case Study — "The Off-Course Golf Course"

IV. Answers to Selected Teaching Activities

# Facts About Water Resources

## Introduction

Water is perhaps our most important natural resource. Without water, life on earth as we know it would cease. During the past several decades, there has been a growing concern in the United States about the proper management of our vital water resources. Water pollution has been a major problem, and recently, certain regions have experienced water shortages. Water resource management will continue to be an important public policy issue. Wise public policy requires citizens and decision makers who are knowledgeable about our water resources and who understand basic economic principles.

## Basic Information

WATER, WATER, EVERYWHERE: Water is certainly a remarkable substance. In addition to being necessary for life itself, water transports people, goods, and waste; defines political boundaries; cools industrial equipment; irrigates crops; provides electricity and recreation; plays a major role in determining the weather; and is the "universal solvent." Given water's importance, it is fortunate that it is so abundant. Indeed, four-fifths of the world's surface is covered with water, and scientists estimate that the total water supply is 396 billion gallons! However, little of this water is usable, since 97 percent is salty ocean water. Another two percent is stored in glaciers and ice caps. In fact, only 0.8 percent of all the earth's water is fresh water that is immediately available for human use. This amount is basically a fixed supply and is all that we have, given the current technology.

FRESH WATER SOURCES: The fresh water that is available for human use exists primarily as surface water or ground water. **Surface water** is water that we can see. There are five basic categories of surface water: rivers and streams, lakes, oceans, estuaries, and wetlands.

- **Rivers and streams** often begin as fresh springs in mountain areas. The springs turn into streams and then into rivers. Some rivers, such as the Mississippi, start from ground water sources. Springs are the natural discharge of ground water to the surface.

- **Lakes** are bodies of water surrounded by a larger land mass. Lakes change as they age, primarily by accumulating sediment from surrounding land areas.

- **Oceans** are large bodies of salt water that cover 66 percent of the earth surface.

- **Estuaries** form where rivers meet oceans. Estuaries are valuable because they are places where many aquatic species breed and live.

- **Wetlands** are low lying areas that are periodically covered with shallow water. Wetlands are natural filters that preserve and protect ground water quality, help control flooding, and are a breeding ground for many species of wildlife.

- **Ground water** is stored underground. Its importance is illustrated by its volume — over 30 times greater than the volume of rivers, streams, and lakes. Most people believe groundwater exists in underground caves. In fact, most ground water is contained in **aquifers,** porous underground areas containing sand or loosely packed granular materials. The size of the material determines the storage capacity of the aquifer **(porosity)** and its ability to transmit ground water **(permeability).** Ground water flow can vary from several feet a day to only inches per year. Aquifers may be near the surface or deep underground. They may be shallow formations or thousands of feet thick. About one-fourth of all the fresh water used in the United States (one half of the drinking water) comes from underground sources. Nearly 60 percent of Indiana's population uses ground water for drinking water.

WATER CYCLE: The amount of water available for human use is being replenished constantly through the **water cycle.** Water evaporates into the atmosphere in the form of water vapor. Only pure water evaporates — solids, impurities, and salts remain behind. Eventually the water vapor cools and falls as fresh water, usually as rain or snow. Most water falls into the oceans. The water that falls on land surfaces either flows into streams and rivers, eventually reaching the oceans, or seeps into the ground and replenishes the groundwater supply. Ground water and surface water interact in the water cycle, as ground water partially recharges rivers, streams, lakes, and oceans. The water cycle is a never-ending process that continually renews the fresh water of the earth.

WATER DISTRIBUTION: One of the unique and challenging features about fresh water availability is its uneven distribution. In some countries and in some regions of the United States, there is an abundant per capita water supply. In other areas, water is much more **scarce.** And yet, human habitation doesn't always correlate with fresh water availability. For example, there is abundant water in the sparsely populated rainforests of South America, but much less water in certain heavily populated regions in the Western United States. These arid regions have continuous or periodic water shortages.

# Water Management Problems

There are two fundamental problems in the area of water resource management: (1) the issue of **pollution** *(quality)* and (2) the issue of **availability** *(quantity).*

WATER POLLUTION: Water pollution is a complex and interesting subject. In general, people want clean water and have strong opinions about water quality. In the 1960s, people became very concerned about the deteriorating quality of water in the United States. Since that time, the water quality has improved throughout much of the country. However, water pollution is still a real problem and is the focus of much public concern.

*Pollution: What is It?* It is important to distinguish between "waste" and "pollution." In nature, all living creatures generate waste. It is best to think of **pollution** as meaning "too much." Too much of anything, including waste products, even if it is **biodegradable**, is not good for the environment. For example, in 1776 the biodegradable waste dumped into the river from small farms was not a problem. The same could not be said today. There are more people, so the sheer quantity of such waste causes a major pollution problem.

*Pollution from Nature:* Water can be polluted by nature as well as by humans. The most common surface water pollution comes from erosion. Soil particles that enter surface water block sunlight and impair photosynthesis, a process plants depend on to survive. Volcanic eruptions and forest fires cause thermal pollution of surface waters. In some areas, high levels of dissolved salts, iron, calcium, or magnesium may make water unsuitable for drinking or other domestic and farming purposes.

*Pollution from Humans:* Any time water is used in production or consumption, its quality changes to some degree. If this change is significant, the water becomes "polluted." Primary sources of pollutants are households, industry, agriculture, municipal landfills, and certain government activities.

*Types of Water Pollution:* There are various basic types of water pollution:

- **Biodegradable Wastes** — Biodegradable wastes, such as sewage and food waste, can harm water supplies because they provide food for oxygen-consuming bacteria. These wastes also contain disease-causing bacteria, viruses, and parasitic worms.

- **Plant Nutrients** — Fertilizers enter waterways primarily from agricultural runoff, causing excessive growth of algae and other water plants. The decomposition of dead plants by bacteria reduces oxygen content and kills certain aquatic populations.

- **Chemical Wastes** — Many different kinds of organic and inorganic chemicals enter our water supplies in a variety of ways. Examples include various toxic wastes, leakage from underground tanks, and pesticides.

- **Heat** — Many large industries use water to cool their machinery. When this heated water is discharged into waterways, it raises overall water temperatures. This reduces dissolved oxygen content and harms certain fish and crustacean populations.

- **Sediments** — Poor soil conservation practices often allow large levels of **silt** to enter waterways. An excessive amount of silt clouds water, limiting the sunlight necessary for photosynthesis by algae and other water plants. When the silt settles to the bottom as **sediment,** it covers the spawning areas of fish and shellfish.

- **Radioactive Materials** — Despite very stiff regulations about radioactive waste disposal, radioactive materials sometimes enter our waterways, primarily through uranium mining, fallout from nuclear testing, and accidental releases.

*Point and Nonpoint Source Pollution:*  The various types of water pollution can be categorized into two major groups:  point source pollution and nonpoint source pollution.  **Point source** pollution enters water resources at a particular site, such as waste water discharged from a pipe or a leak in an underground gasoline storage tank.  **Nonpoint source** pollution comes from discharges from large land areas.  Examples include runoff from croplands, construction areas, parking lots, and urban areas.  The distinction requires different public policy approaches to find effective solutions.

WATER AVAILABILITY:  In certain arid areas with rapidly growing populations, water availability *is* a serious problem. In arid regions that rely heavily on agriculture, such as California, the problem is even more acute because of the huge amount of water needed for irrigation.  Local and state governments are developing public policies to deal with this problem.  This is difficult because of the conflicting interests of groups competing for the right to use the scarce water resources.

# Dealing with Water Pollution

Nobody wants polluted water resources.  People want their water resources to be clean and safe.  But if water quality is so important, why has water pollution been such a problem?  Why are solutions to water pollution sometimes so controversial?

WHO OWNS THE WATER?  Water can be found throughout the United States; in fact, we have over 250,000 rivers!  You have already learned what an important and scarce resource water is to humans.  So who owns the water?

In the settlement of America, the government did not play a large role in **property rights**; rather, it was up to settlers to claim their property.  Since water was a significant factor in the development of towns, the first settlements were usually located near bodies of water.  This accounts for the curved shapes of states in the humid East and along the coasts where there are many rivers.  The property rights regime associated with this type of settlement is called **riparian rights**, which give the right to use the water to the owner of the land adjacent to the body of water.  This method of allocation made sense because those that owned land near the water had easy access.  However, the population of the United States has increased since the time of settlement making this form of water allocation no longer acceptable.

Since a riparian right tied the rights of water to the land, the rights could not be separately transferred to people that needed water, but not land.  The **prior-appropriation doctrine** was developed to solve this problem of water transferability by giving the right of the water to the first person to use the resource, regardless of land ownership.  This allowed private companies to construct irrigation systems, which helped agriculture and mining flourish in the arid Western states, whose rectangular boundaries are not water-based.

Currently, both state and federal governments play a large role in the allocation of water. In the 1860s, states began to claim ownership of bodies of water, which gave people a **usufruct right**, the right to use water rather than to own the water. This public ownership allowed the government to control the rates charged by companies for irrigation. When it became necessary for water to be transferred across state boundaries, the federal government became involved in water rights to promote fairness and efficiency in regional development and economic growth.

Since 1900, the federal government has built almost 700 dams to provide water and power to the West. Much of the water used by localities and for development is subsidized by the federal government. For example, 81 percent of the cost of supplying irrigation water and 64 percent of municipal water costs are paid by the federal government.

THE PROBLEM OF SPILLOVER EFFECTS: The major economic reason why water pollution is a problem is that most water resources are commonly owned, and are, therefore, overused. For example, a company located on a river has an economic incentive to use the river (or the air) for waste disposal because there is no immediate cost for doing so. This probably would not be a problem if only one company put waste in the river; but if many companies use the river for waste disposal, the water quality deteriorates rapidly.

The harmful effects of the pollution of commonly owned resources are called **spillover costs,** or **external costs.** These harmful effects are imposed on other people, forcing these "innocent bystanders" to bear some of the costs of production. For example, instead of incurring the production costs of treating waste water properly, a company can shift these costs to others in the form of polluted water. This is the rationale for government getting involved in pollution control. Through regulation, taxation, or other means, the government attempts to force *internalization* of the negative external effects of pollution. (For a more complete discussion of spillover effects see pages 10-12.)

THE PROBLEM OF SCARCITY: At first glance, improving water quality seems simple enough — the government should implement various regulatory policies that keep people from polluting. Unfortunately, the solution is not that straightforward. Water is required in all production and consumption activities; and any time water is used, its quality is affected to some degree. The only way to guard our water resources completely from pollution would be to stop using them altogether — hardly a feasible solution! The real issue to consider in public policy decisions is *how* clean we want our water to be. Perfection isn't possible.

At the heart of this issue is the problem of **scarcity.** It takes scarce productive resources (natural, human, and capital) to ensure a safe and clean water supply. These same production resources also can be used for a variety of other valuable purposes. A community that devotes productive resources to water quality must give up the opportunity of using these resources for other things, such as better roads, schools, and police protection.

HOW CLEAN IS CLEAN? How does a community or society determine how many productive resources to devote to water quality, or to any other energy or environmental problem? The economic concept of marginalism helps to answer this question. (See page 13 for a more complete discussion of marginalism.) The basic idea of "optimality" is that, after some point, it is not wise to devote additional productive resources to water quality since the additional costs of continuing to improve water quality become greater than the additional benefits. After some point, it is better to devote scarce productive resources to other valuable purposes. Marginal analysis includes careful consideration of monetary estimates of the costs and benefits of policy options. This can be difficult, especially assigning monetary values to things such as the recreational and aesthetic value of clean water. For different people, these values will vary. Despite the difficulties, marginal analysis gives policymakers their best tool in analyzing energy and environmental issues.

HOW MUCH IS DANGEROUS? Scientists have made great strides in their ability to detect minute levels of possibly dangerous chemicals in our water supplies. For example, in the 1950s, scientists could detect chemicals in water at the part per million (ppm) level. By 1975, this had dropped to parts per trillion (ppt), and recently scientists have found some chemicals at the part per quadrillion (ppq) level! However, these technological advances can complicate public policy decisions. While we now can detect chemicals previously not thought to be in our water supplies, we lack scientific data confirming how these minute quantities affect human health and the environment.

For example, ground water sometimes contains minute quantities of pesticides that leak into the ground. These quantities are usually detected at levels of parts per billion (ppb), a level equivalent to one ounce of chemical dissolved in one billion ounces of water. (One ppb is approximately equal to dissolving one-sixth of an aspirin tablet in 16,000 gallons of water, approximately the amount of liquid held in a large train tank car.) Is water containing these minute quantities of these chemicals unsafe? In many cases, we simply don't know. However, this illustrates the importance of dosage levels when defining pollution. For example, substances such as chlorine and fluoride are considered toxic at rather modest levels, yet we *add* them to our water supplies to kill harmful microorganisms and reduce tooth decay.

HOW SAFE IS OUR WATER? Since the 1970s, water quality has improved significantly in the United States, thanks in part to federal legislation, such as the Clean Water Act of 1972 and the Safe Drinking Water Act (SDWA) of 1974. These acts charge the Environmental Protection Agency (EPA) with monitoring overall water quality. The SDWA established national water standards called maximum containment levels, or MCLs, for any pollutants that "may" have negative effects on human health. Public water supplies must monitor and comply with these standards. Individuals with private water supplies are responsible for monitoring the quality of their own water. The Clean Water Act and other acts required the EPA to establish national effluent standards and to monitor the amounts of contaminants entering our waterways.

Since 1999, states have been required to develop and implement standards of water quality. These values, known as the Water Quality Standards, represent the maximum allowable levels of various contaminants that may exist in the water without causing serious human health problems. To comply with the Clean Water Act, states are required to assess the quality of all bodies of water regarding these standards.

If the actual concentration of any particular contaminant exceeds the standard in a given water body, the water body is deemed to be impaired with respect to that pollutant. The state is required to develop and implement specific plans for attaining Total Maximum Daily Loads, commonly known as TMDLs, for all impaired water bodies. These are calculations of the maximum amount of specific pollutants that a particular body of water can receive in one day and still remain within the standard.

Experts agree that many water supplies in the United States are generally safe for their intended purposes. However, this issue will remain a source of controversy since some level of contamination is inevitable and individuals will disagree on the effects of minute quantities of contaminants that now can be detected.

# Dealing with Water Availability

TWO GENERAL APPROACHES: There are various regions in the western United States that have too little water. This is due largely to low and variable precipitation, high runoff evaporation rates, depletion of ground water supplies because of intensive irrigation, and increased demands from a growing population. There are two basic approaches to dealing with water availability problems: (1) increase **supply** and/or (2) reduce **demand.**

INCREASING SUPPLY: There are various ways to increase water supplies. One of the primary ways is to build dams and reservoirs, which collect water and store it for dry periods, provide flood control, and are a source of energy for electric generation. However, dams and reservoirs are costly to build and they must also be kept free from silt, which can disrupt a river's ecological balance.

Water diversion projects transfer water from one watershed to another, but they are expensive and may have harmful environmental impacts. Another alternative is to rely more heavily on ground water sources. This also can be a problem because excessive usage leads to aquifer depletion. Less feasible alternatives include clouding, seeding, and desalination, which are quite expensive.

REDUCING DEMAND: There are two primary ways to reduce water usage. The first is to conserve water by promoting better **water efficiency.** Water efficiency measures how much water it takes to do a certain task. Because water has been generally plentiful and inexpensive in the United States, water efficiency has not been a major concern. Industry, agriculture, and households have tended to use large amounts of water. There has been an emphasis recently to improve water efficiency in all areas. Many industries now recycle waste water for reuse and use new manufacturing techniques to conserve water. In agriculture, new irrigation techniques reduce evaporation and seepage. Many households now have water-saving fixtures and devices that significantly reduce water usage.

The second basic way to reduce water usage is through **full-cost pricing.** Because of government subsidies and pricing policies, the price of water is often kept artificially low and does not reflect the true relative scarcity of water. For example, residential water meters frequently use "decreasing block" pricing, which charges a lower rate for successive units (volume discounts per each hundred gallons per week) rather than "increasing block" pricing, where citizens pay more as they use more water. Low prices encourage consumption and reduce water efficiency. In some regions, consumers are not even metered for their water usage. The obvious economic solution is to establish a true market price for water. Politically, however, this can be difficult. Consumers, especially western farmers, depend heavily on supplies of cheap water. Water pricing and the parallel issue of water rights will remain important and controversial issues.

# Summary

Is there really a water crisis in the United States, as many news stories indicate? In general, experts agree that there is no immediate crisis in water quality or availability. For the most part, water supplies in the United States are adequate, and the quality is suitable for desired purposes. However, average national statistics mask real local and regional problems. Most experts believe that the water management policies of the federal government, which previously focused on national standards, are shifting to accommodate these local and regional needs. As one report stated:

> Because water management problems and concerns are increasingly localized and complex, the focus of policy decision making is now shifting to non-Federal levels. Where nationally consistent policies were appropriate to water quality or resource management in the past, today's problems require more finely tuned responses.... These may take the form of supplementing national policies with flexibility to address local considerations or even of defining what is "national" in terms of diverse regional or local solutions to a particular water management problem.[1]

One thing is certain - water management issues will figure prominently in public policy decisions in the years ahead.

---

1. "An overview of the Nation's Water," *World Eagle*, (March 1992), p. 33.

# Teaching Activities

# Teaching Instructions

## Overview:

The specific teaching activities do not have to be done in order. However, you will probably want to do the Case Studies toward the end of the units, after students have mastered much of the basic information. Some of the basic information to teach your students is found in the preceding *Facts About Water Resources* section. Other information is available from a variety of sources, many of which are listed in the *Resources* section. Encourage your students to research information on their own. The Further Explorations Activity suggests a variety of research activities.

Some of the key economic concepts your students should learn in this unit on water resources are described immediately below in the Key Concepts to Emphasize. These concepts are also highlighted in the Key Questions to Ask Students part of the specific teaching activities.

## Key Concepts to Emphasize

1.  **All Water is "Polluted" to Some Degree:** In nature, there is no such thing as "pure" water. According to the Environmental Protection Agency (EPA), "Probably one of the most important and basic concepts to understand about the earth's water is that it is not pure." This is because water readily dissolves both natural and man-made substances.

2.  **"The Dose Makes the Poison":** Whether water is safe depends primarily on the *amount* (not merely the existence) of a pollutant in the water. According to the EPA, "The level or quantity of a substance in water is the central issue with respect to determining whether the water is adequate for human consumption."

3.  **Making Water Perfectly Clean Is Not Wise Public Policy:** How clean *should* our water be? This question is the crux of the water pollution issue. Economists argue that it makes sense to clean up water resources to the point where the additional (marginal) benefits of the purer water equal the additional (marginal) costs. Beyond that point, further cleanup is unwise since scarce productive resources could best be used elsewhere, such as for better roads, schools, medical research, etc.

4.  **The Role of Price in Water Issues:** Water is not a free good. It takes scarce productive resources to supply clean, safe water for people to use. The price of a good reflects its relative scarcity. In arid regions, water is more scarce and should be more expensive. If the price of water truly reflects its scarcity, there will be no water shortages. However, if governments keep the price artificially low (below the true market price), too much water will be used, resulting in shortages, as there are out west.

5.  **Progress in Managing Water Resources:** In the past 30 years, the quality of water resources in the United States has improved substantially. This improvement reflects a better control of point source pollution. More attention is now being given to the management of nonpoint pollution sources.

# Activity 1
## The Water Cycle Game:  Along for the Ride!

**Teaching Objectives:**

After completing this activity/game, students will be able to:

1.  Explain how water is constantly renewed through the water cycle processes of evaporation, condensation, precipitation, and accumulation.
2.  Identify various stages in the water cycle where water can be polluted.
3.  Explain that most of the water we use is "polluted" to some degree.

**Time Allowed:**    40 minutes

**Materials:**
- Water Cycle game board
- Pollution cards
- Raindrop markers
- One die

**Vocabulary/Concepts:**

- *Aquifer:*  porous underground layers of sand or other granular materials that hold ground water
- *Biosphere:*  the part of the earth and its atmosphere where life exists
- *Condensation:*  the changing of a gas to a liquid
- *Evaporation:*  liquid turning into a gas
- *Groundwater:*  water located beneath the earth's surface
- *Pollutant:*  any substance that dirties the environment
- *Precipitation:*  rain, snow, or other forms of water that fall to the earth
- *Scarcity:*  the condition, at a zero price, of not having all of the goods, services, or productive resources (including water) that you want
- *Surface Water:*  water one can see, including oceans, rivers, lakes, estuaries, and wetlands
- *Sediment:*  material that settles to the bottom of a liquid
- *Transpiration:*  the giving off of moisture through skin pores or leaves
- *Water Cycle:*  movement of water in our environment as it goes from liquid to vapor and back to liquid again
- *Water Table:*  upper surface of an underground area that is completely saturated with water

Water is essential to all life on earth.  The human body is more than 60 percent water.  Water flows in our veins as well as in the sap in trees.  There is a finite amount of water on earth.  The same molecule of water has gone through millions of changes through the ages.  In nature, water purifies itself by **evaporating** and leaving impurities behind.  However, when too many **pollutants** enter the cycle, it is difficult for them to be removed naturally.

## Teaching Procedure:

Background:  To prepare students for playing the Water Cycle Game, write and circle the words **"Water Cycle"** on a large piece of paper.  Ask students to share any associations they have concerning this concept.  (*What do you think of when you hear these words?*)  Record all responses in a web-like pattern/concept map.  Keep the responses on display throughout all water activities.  When the responses need to be expanded or altered, use a different colored marker.

Explain the natural water cycle, defining the processes of **evaporation, condensation, precipitation,** and **accumulation.**  (See Vocabulary and *Facts About Water Resources.*)

Discuss the concept of water pollution.  List the various **types of water pollution** (page 102) and identify specific **pollutants.**  Identify where these pollutants enter the water cycle.  (*water vapor combining with emissions to create acid rain; point source discharges from factories or waste from disposal sites; sediment from agriculture, construction, or timber harvesting; oil and chemical surface runoff; toxic wastes from mining, old storage tanks, or landfills, etc.*)

Playing the Game:  Each student becomes a "raindrop" and takes a journey around the water cycle.  During the journey, players pass through pollution areas and must pick up pollution cards.  At designated points, players can "drop" some of the pollutants.  The raindrop that successfully travels one complete turn of the cycle while collecting the least number of pollution cards is declared the "Top Drop."

1.  Place each set of four Pollution Cards face down on one of the four "Pollution Entry Clouds" in each corner of the game board according to the designated type of pollution.

2.  Randomly choose a "Starter" to begin the game.  Play proceeds to the Starter's left.  The Starter places a raindrop on the "Start" square, rolls a die, and moves in the direction of the arrow, simulating the path of water in the cycle.  More than one marker may occupy a space.

3.  The squares marked E (evaporation), C/P (condensation/precipitation), A (accumulation), or GW (ground water) indicate where pollution can enter the water cycle.  A player landing on one of these squares must draw the appropriate card, identify the pollutant out loud, and keep the pollutant until the end of the game.  A player landing on a "Drop Out" or "Filter Out" square may return a pollution card to the appropriate "Pollution Entry Cloud."  Play continues until all raindrops pass the "Finish" square.  The player with the least number of pollution cards is declared "Top Drop."  In the case of a tie, players continue for one more cycle.

## Teaching Tips:

1.  Prepare at least two sets of "Pollution Cards" for each game board used.  Laminate Pollution Cards and Raindrop Markers to enhance durability.

## Key Questions To Ask Students:

1. Name the different forms water takes as it travels through the water cycle. (*liquid, vapor, ice*)

2. How does the water cycle purify our water? (*When water evaporates, it leaves impurities behind and precipitates in a cleaner form.*)

3. Is water always "polluted?" (*Yes, it is always polluted to some degree, although that degree will vary.*)

4. Is water that has tiny amounts of pollutants dangerous? (*Not necessarily. No water is completely pure; there are trace elements of "pollutants" in virtually all water. It is the "dose that makes the poison;" that is, the concentration of the pollutants is really crucial.*)

## Bulletin Board Ideas:

1. Enlarge a map of the earth and use different colors to shade in the areas of the earth according to amounts of rainfall.

## Student Journal Ideas:

1. Contact your local utility company to find out the source of your local water supply. Then have students pretend they are a drop of water that has just entered your school. Have students write and illustrate a story about the previous experience of the water drop, including details of how it managed to stay so clean.

2. Identify ways that humans influence how water moves through the water cycle. (*humidifiers and dehumidifiers, watering lawns, transporting water long distances, returning water to waterways after sewage treatment, steam turbines to make electricity, etc.*)

EVAPORATION

CONDENSATION
PRECIPITATION

Pollution in

PRECIPITATION

CONDENSATION

DROP OUT

EVAPORATION

TRAPPED
IN ICE
LOSE TURN

ACCUMULATION

DROP OUT

GROUNDWATER

START

the water cycle

FILTER OUT

FILTER OUT

FILTER OUT

ALONG
FOR THE RIDE!

GROUNDWATER

ACCUMULATION

KEY:
C/P = CONDENSATION/PRECIPITATION        E = EVAPORATION
GW = GROUNDWATER                        A= ACCUMULATION

**Pollution Cards: Paste corresponding answers (next page) on back of cards.**

**GAME PIECES:** Fold along dotted line to stand up.

| | | | |
|---|---|---|---|
| **(C/P)**<br>**FACTORY**<br>**SMOKESTACK**<br>**WITH NO**<br>**SCRUBBERS** | **(C/P)**<br>**CAR AND**<br>**TRUCK**<br>**EXHAUST** | **(C/P)**<br>**BURNING OF**<br>**OIL FIELDS** | **(C/P)**<br>**COAL**<br>**FURNACE**<br>**IN**<br>**OLDER HOME** |
| **(E)**<br>**TOXIC**<br>**PESTICIDE**<br>**SPRAY IN AIR** | **(E)**<br>**EXHAUST**<br>**FROM**<br>**AIRPLANE**<br>**ENGINE** | **(E)**<br>**VOLCANIC**<br>**ASHES** | **(E)**<br>**DUST**<br>**PARTICLES** |
| **(G/W)**<br>**LANDFILL**<br>**SEEPAGE** | **(G/W)**<br>**LEAKY SEPTIC**<br>**TANK** | **(G/W)**<br>**USED OIL**<br>**FROM CAR**<br>**ENGINE** | **(G/W)**<br>**SALT WATER**<br>**SEEPAGE** |
| **(A)**<br>**CATTLE**<br>**GRAZING**<br>**NEAR STREAM** | **(A)**<br>**EROSION FROM**<br>**TOO MUCH**<br>**LOGGING** | **(A)**<br>**DISCHARGES**<br>**FROM**<br>**FACTORIES** | **(A)**<br>**FERTILIZER**<br>**RUN OFF**<br>**FROM**<br>**FARM FIELDS** |

# Activity 2
## Putting Hard Water to the Test

**Teaching Objectives:** After completing this activity, students will be able to:

1. Explain the difference between "hard" and "soft" water.
2. Identify productive resources needed to soften water.
3. Identify opportunity costs and trade-offs in choices involving hard and soft water.

**Time Allowed:**     40 minutes

**Materials (per group):**

- baby food jar with lid
- plastic cup with pin holes in bottom
- limestone chips (finely ground)
- 100 ml rainwater (or bottled water)
- coffee filter
- 1/4 teaspoon powdered laundry soap

**Vocabulary/Concepts:**

- *Hard/soft water:* a measure of the presence or absence of minerals such as calcium, magnesium, and iron
- *Opportunity Cost:* the value of one's next best alternative when making a decision
- *Trade-off:* giving up some of one thing in order to get some of another

**Teaching Procedure:**

1. Review basic facts about ground water from the *Facts About Water Resources* section. Explain that although ground water is relatively free of pollutants, it contains naturally dissolved materials such as calcium, magnesium, and iron that affect water usability. Discuss the hardness and softness of water, and the reasons and ways that people soften their water.

2. Explain that water can be tested for hardness by adding powdered laundry soap and shaking. Demonstrate by pouring 100 ml of rainwater into a baby food jar. Add a pinch of laundry soap. Secure the lid and shake the jar 15 times. Mark the height of the lather, and set the jar aside as the "control sample."

3. Break into teams to investigate how the hardness/softness of rainwater is affected as it seeps into aquifers. Follow these procedures:

   a. Obtain the listed materials
   b. Place a coffee filter inside the plastic cup and add the limestone chips.
   c. Slowly pour 100 ml of rainwater through the cup/filter/chips into one of the jars.
   d. Add a pinch of laundry soap to the water and secure the lid.

e. Predict the height of the lather.

f. Shake 15 times. Compare the height of the lather with that of the "control jar."

g. Discuss the results.

4. Explain that rainwater is considered "soft." When rainwater seeps through the ground on its way to aquifers, it dissolves minerals such as the calcium found in limestone and becomes "hard." Soft water will maintain a significant lather; hard water will not. Did student investigations confirm this?

## Teaching Tips:

1. With certain kinds of limestone, not enough calcium may dissolve to give the water enough hardness. To remedy this, use a weak vinegar solution (25 ml vinegar/100 ml rainwater) to help dissolve the calcium. The vinegar simply helps calcium to dissolve; it does not, in itself, contribute to water hardness. To prove this, add the soap powder to the vinegar/rainwater solution alone and test for hardness. It should still be soft.

2. Another way to increase calcium without using vinegar is to let the water stand overnight in a cup of limestone chips.

## Key Questions To Ask Students:

1. What makes water "hard?" (*minerals such as calcium, iron, and manganese*)

2. What scarce productive resources does it take to soften water to make it more usable? (*natural resources – rock salt, metals; human resources – expertise and labor to create and install softening systems; capital resources – water softeners, pipes, tools, etc.*)

3. What costs/expenses are there if someone doesn't soften water? (*minerals collect on pipes, in appliances, etc.*)

4. Mrs. Brown has saved $400 to buy <u>either</u> a water softener or a new large freezer. If she buys the softener, what is her opportunity cost? (*the freezer*) If she buys the freezer, what is her opportunity cost? (*the softener*)

5. What are the trade-offs in Mrs. Brown's decision? (*trading off the benefits of softer water for the benefits of being able to freeze more food*)

## Bulletin Board Ideas:

1. Illustrate how rainwater becomes hardened as it passes through the ground to aquifers.

2. Show the opportunity cost of Mrs. Brown's softener/freezer decision.

## Student Journal Ideas:

1. Write and illustrate a paragraph entitled: "How Rainwater Becomes Hard."

2. Write a paragraph entitled "The Costs and Benefits of Soft Water."

# Activity 3
## Does Clean Mean Pristine?

**Teaching Objectives:** After completing this activity, students will:

1. Understand that it is costly to clean the environment.
2. Explain that individuals usually clean the environment by doing the least costly activities first.
3. Explain why it is too expensive, in terms of opportunity cost, to have "perfectly" clean water.
4. Formulate a personal definition of "clean water," and understand that individuals differ on their definition of a clean environment.

**Time Allowed:**     30-40 minutes

**Materials:**     Materials representing various "pollutants" found in water (such as scrap papers, popcorn, wood shavings, small dots from the paper punch, plastic, rice, grains of sand, glitter, dried grits, etc.)

**Vocabulary/Concepts:**

- *Capital Resources:* physical goods, such as tools, buildings, and equipment, which are used to produce other goods or services

- *Opportunity Cost:* the value of one's best alternative when making a decision

- *Water Pollution:* harmful or unwanted effects on waterways caused by contaminants and waste

Individuals usually agree that water quality is a problem that needs to be addressed. However, they frequently do not agree on the *degree* of water quality. In other words, how clean is clean? Students learn an important economic concept – that the **opportunity cost** of continuing to clean up contaminated water eventually becomes too great. At some point, the extra (marginal) effort and cost required for additional cleanup is not worth the benefits. When this point is reached, the **scarce productive resources** used for cleanup would best be used elsewhere.

**Teaching Procedure:**

1. While students are out of the room, litter the floor with a variety of different-sized "water polluting" materials. (See materials list.) Be sure to include a significant amount of tiny, "difficult-to-pick-up" materials, such as sand, glitter, or dried grits.

2. When students arrive, explain that the items on the floor represent different water pollutants in a nearby pond. Since the pond is a source of water and recreation for the community, it is important to reduce the level of pollution immediately!

3. Allow three approximately one-minute rounds to clean up the "pond." After each round, record on the board the types of "pollution" that were found. Discuss what types of water pollution each item could represent. By the end of the third round, the obvious pollutants should be gone and the pond should be "clean."

4. After the third round ask, "Now have we cleaned up our pond?" After students agree, examine the floor carefully and discover some small bits of glitter, sand, dust, etc. Tell students that the pond is *not* clean since some tiny pollutants remain. Ask if students want to continue cleaning the pond. (They won't want to!)

5. Be sure to ask the Key Questions below.

## Teaching Tips:

1. Be sure to distribute enough water "pollutants" – large and small. You'll be surprised at how well 25 students can clean up a classroom in three minutes.

2. To simplify the activity, have a smaller group of students do the cleanup.

## Key Questions to Ask Students:

1. What types of water "pollutants" did you find? (*biodegradable – paper, wood shavings, rice, etc.; nonbiodegradable – plastic, metal, glitter, etc.*) Could there be some left we cannot see? (*yes, dissolved substances and chemicals.*)

2. What did you have to do to "clean up" the water? (*We had to work, which took energy and time. To do a thorough job, we needed <u>capital</u>, such as a broom or vacuum cleaner. In real life, it would take scarce <u>productive resources</u> to clean up water.*)

3. What types of pollutants did you remove first? Why? (*large items. They were less costly to remove in terms of time and energy. The benefit was also greatest – it looked cleaner sooner.*)

4. Why did you conclude that the water was "clean" when it actually wasn't? (*It appeared to be clean; it was clean enough. Only tiny pollutants, such as glitter, remained.*)

5. Why don't we spend more time cleaning up the remaining pollutants? (*It would take too much time. The <u>opportunity cost</u> is too great. We have other more important things to do!*)

6. In real public policy, such as the Safe Water Drinking Act, why doesn't the government take more drastic action to enforce even stricter safe water drinking standards? (*The marginal cost of doing so would probably exceed the marginal benefits. Scarce productive resources would be better used for other priorities, such as better education, roads, cancer research, etc.*)

7. After concluding the first round, was the room ("pond") clean enough for some people but not for others? (*yes*) Is your room at home ever clean enough for you but not for your parents? (*yes! One of the difficulties of solving environmental problems is that people have different tolerance levels for pollution.*)

## Bulletin Board Idea:

1. Determine where your community is located on the earth map from the Bulletin Board Idea in Activity 1. Place one end of a piece of yarn on that spot and attach the other end to an enlarged "insert" map of your community. Highlight a lake, pond, or stream nearby. Have the students study the surrounding area and identify the watershed (all the land that drains into a particular body of water) for the highlighted water. Make "pollution cards" representing different types of pollution that might be contaminating the highlighted water. Mount the cards on water drops and place them around the community map.

## Student Journal Ideas:

1. Take a walk around your community.

2. Have students record any potential water pollution problems encountered during the walk by taking pictures or drawing representative sketches.

3. Discuss what is causing the potential water pollution problem.

4. Have students write an imaginary letter from the Environmental Protection Agency (EPA) to the alleged polluter. The letter should outline the pollution problem, explain the possible harm to the community, and offer possible solutions to the problem, noting the opportunity costs of any course of action.

(An original version of this activity appeared in the article "A Clean Environment, A Matter of Choice," by Robert W. Reinke and Diane W. Reinke, in the *Elementary Economist*, Spring 1989.)

# Activity 4
## Decision Time in Bonedry, California

**Teaching Objectives:** After completing this activity, students will be able to:

1. Draw a diagram illustrating the distribution of the earth's water supply.

2. Explain why fresh water is a scarce good.

3. Explain how prices reflect relative scarcity.

4. Apply the concept of water conservation (water efficiency) to their daily lives.

**Time Allowed:** 30-40 minutes

**Materials:**
- Where in the World Is the Water? handout
- Decision Time in Bonedry, CA worksheet
- Decision Tree or Five Step Model handouts (pages 19-20)

## Vocabulary/Concepts:

- *Scarcity:* the condition of not being able to have all of the goods, services, or productive resources that you want. Water is considered *scarce* because it's not freely available in unlimited quantities.

- *Price:* the amount people pay to buy a good, service, or productive resource. Prices reflect *relative scarcity.* Items which are relatively more scarce generally cost more than those which are not.

- *Water Conservation:* a general term describing the wise and efficient use of water resources

Fresh water is considered a **scarce good** because it is not freely available in unlimited quantities. It takes scarce **productive resources** to provide adequate and safe water, and people, therefore, have to pay to obtain it. The **price** of water reflects its relative scarcity. Fortunately, even though fresh water comprises only a small fraction of total worldwide water supplies, there is an abundant supply available to meet most human needs and wants. This is why the price of water, perhaps our most valuable natural resource, is so very low. In arid regions, raising the price of water can make water use more efficient and help improve **water conservation.**

## Teaching Procedure:

1. Discuss the distribution of water on the earth's surface. (See *Facts About Water Resources.*) Emphasize that fresh water supplies are generally adequate, but unevenly distributed, causing regional and local water problems.

2. Have students complete the Where in the World is the Water? handout. Discuss the issue of water availability/scarcity. (Use Key Questions To Ask Students below.)

3. Read and discuss the Decision Time in Bonedry, CA worksheet scenario. Role-play how different individuals (farmers, elderly people with low incomes, wealthy people with swimming pools, etc.) might react to the new water policies.

4. Next, divide students into groups of three or four. Use the Decision Tree or Five Step decision models to solve the water problem on the Decision Time in Bonedry, California worksheet. Discuss the group decisions.

5. Review all Key Questions To Ask Students below.

**Key Questions to Ask Students:**

1. Why is fresh water considered a *scarce* good? (*It is not freely available in unlimited supplies. We have to pay to get it.*)

2. What scarce productive resources are necessary to produce clean, safe water? (*Water treatment plants, pipes, equipment, skilled water specialists to test and provide the water, etc.*)

3. Develop a plan for arid countries to get water from the polar ice caps. Be sure to consider all the scarce productive resources that would be needed. Why don't countries do this now?

# Where In the World Is the Water?

Even though four-fifths of the earth's surface is covered with water, not all water is usable.

Look at the chart below. Decide where each water source is located on the water drop graph. Color each area as directed.

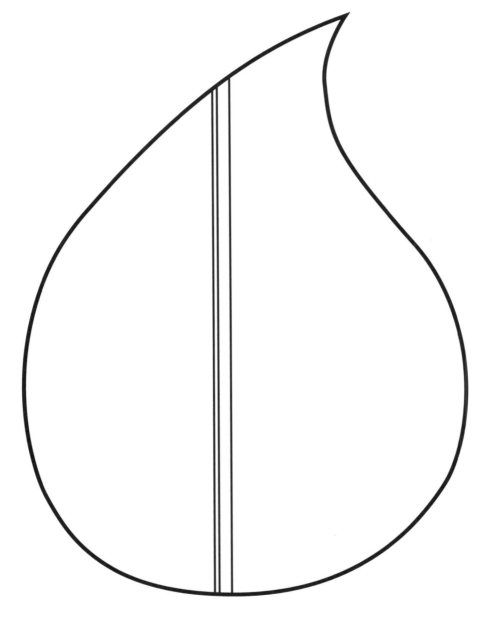

| | | |
|---|---|---|
| Salty Ocean Water | 97% | Orange |
| Polar Ice Caps and Glaciers | 2% | Red |
| Fresh Water (Rivers, Lakes, Ground Water, etc. | <1% | Blue |

# Decision Time in Bonedry, CA

The farming community of Bonedry, California has a problem. Due to a drought and the large irrigation needs of farmers, the fresh water supplies are drying up. To protect the remaining water supplies, the city council conducted a survey to find out what new policy the citizens wanted. After much debate, this notice was sent.

---

TO:    **Citizens of Bonedry**
FROM:   **Bonedry City Council**
REGARDING: **Water Shortage Problem**

The City Council has decided to adopt a new water policy. We have decided to either:

1. Raise the price of water so people will use less OR
2. Ration water (Allow individuals, especially farmers, to use only a limited amount.)

We value your input. Come to the council meeting next week and tell us which policy to adopt. The situation is critical, and something must be done. We will vote on this issue in two weeks.

---

1. What is the **scarcity** problem in Bonedry? _____
_____
_____

2. The Council thinks raising the **price** of water will cause people to use less. Do you agree? Explain. _____
_____
_____

3. Which people in the community might be hurt *most* by the higher prices? Who might be hurt *least?* Explain. _____
_____
_____

4. Who in the community might be hurt *most* and *least* by the rationing plan?
_____
_____

5.  If the City Council votes to ration water, citizens will have to use less. List five ways the citizens could limit water usage in their homes.

_____

_____

_____

_____

_____

6.  What does your group think the City Council should do? How would your group vote? Use the Decision Tree or the Five Step Decision Model to help you decide.

# Activity 5
## Is Cleaning Hazardous to Your Health?

**Teaching Objectives:** After completing this activity, students will be able to:

1. Explain that chemicals from households don't just "go away" – they are deposited somewhere.

2. Identify the opportunity costs and trade-offs of using commercial cleaning products containing toxic chemicals instead of "environmentally friendly" natural substances.

3. Explain that minute amounts of "hazardous" substances may not be dangerous.

**Time Allowed:** 50-60 minutes

**Materials:**
- Examples of commercial products containing toxic substances
- Commercial product for removing tarnish
- Per group:   3-4 tarnished pennies
  1-2 new, shiny pennies
  3 Tbsp white vinegar
  1 Tbsp salt
  1 plastic cup and stirrer
  Decision Tree handout (page 19)
- Is Cleaning Hazardous to Your Health handout

## Vocabulary/Concepts:

- *Opportunity Cost:* the value of one's best alternative when making a decision
- *Nonpoint Water Pollution:* pollution that does not enter surface water at any one point
- *Toxic:* poisonous
- *Trade-Off:* giving up some of one thing in order to get some of another

The earth's water is not completely pure. Contaminants occur naturally in water. They also enter water supplies from nonpoint pollution sources such as household drains and surface runoff from agricultural and urban areas. It is difficult to monitor this type of pollution, and it is also difficult to determine whether or not minute quantities of toxic chemical substances in water supplies are actually harmful. Not using these chemical substances would help the environment to some degree, but would it be worth giving up all the benefits these chemicals provide?

## Teaching Procedure:

1.  Introduce the concept of "toxic." Show several examples of household products containing toxic substances. Have students identify other products and list them on the board. List how these products are helpful in the home.

2.  Discuss the issue of disposal of these toxic substances. (If time permits, research some of the chemical properties of the toxic substances.) Where do they go after they are used? (*down drains, in the air*) Is it dangerous putting these chemicals down drains? Will our water supplies become contaminated? (*This depends on two key factors: a. the <u>toxicity</u> of a substance and b. the <u>quantity</u> of the substance. Even a highly toxic substance is not dangerous in minute concentrations. As the EPA states, "The level or quantity of a substance in water is the central issue with respect to determining whether the water is adequate for human consumption."*)

3.  Discuss how the disposal of toxic substances could be a problem. (*if enough toxic substances were disposed of to bring toxic concentrations in water supplies to dangerous levels.*)

4.  (Optional) Clean a tarnished penny using a commercial product. Does it do a good job? List the chemical ingredients in the commercial product. Are any of them toxic?

5.  Introduce the idea of using nonhazardous cleaning substitutes in the home instead of products containing toxic substances. Give students the "Is Cleaning Hazardous to Your Health?" handout. Divide the class into groups and have them perform the investigation, making sure all students are involved. Have students complete questions 1-6. (Note: To get the pennies shiny in question 4, rub them with a cloth or paper towel.)

6.  When the students are finished, discuss student responses to questions 1-5. Explain that the chemical name for vinegar is acetic acid and for salt is sodium chloride. When mixed, they form a mild solution of hydrochloric acid, which removes the tarnish from the pennies (along with some rubbing!). Hydrochloric acid can be very corrosive, but is also a natural chemical found in the human stomach. It is easily neutralized and isn't toxic in diluted form.

7.  Finally, use the Decision Tree model (in large or small groups) to answer question 6.

## Teaching Tip:

1.  Students may identify more than the two alternatives given in question 6. Students can analyze more than two alternatives by using the Five-Step decision model.

## Key Questions To Ask Students:

1.  Is the earth's water pure? (*No. It contains many dissolved microbiological and chemical contaminants that occur naturally or are caused by human activity.*)

2. What determines whether water is safe to drink or use? *(a. the toxicity of a contaminating substance, and b. the concentration level of that substance.)*

3. What can we do in our homes to help keep our water supplies safe? *(Answers will vary. Try to avoid using toxic chemicals because the cumulative effect can cause problems.)*

4. What are some of your choices when making a decision about a tarnish problem? *(Don't clean, clean with a commercial product, clean with nontoxic substitutes, etc.)*

5. What are the trade-offs involved in deciding whether or not to use a nontoxic substitute instead of a commercial product? *(trading off the benefits of the substitute – more "friendly" for the environment and less costly in terms of money spent. For the benefits of using the commercial product – less time and elbow grease and often a better job of cleaning.)*

6. What are some other nontoxic cleaning substitutes you can use in your house? *(vinegar and water as window cleaner; vinegar and liquid detergent as bathroom sink and tub cleaner; detergent, borax, and lemon juice as toilet bowl cleaner; soap and hydrogen peroxide as disinfectant)*

## Bulletin Board Ideas:

1. Cut out water drops on colored construction paper. Along the top border of the bulletin board, place the following title on some of the drops: "Dropping the Cost of Water Pollution." Whenever students try a substitute for a product containing toxic substances, write down the idea on a new water drop and add it to the bulletin board.

## Student Journal Ideas:

1. Write a paragraph explaining why you agree or disagree with this sentence: "If a toxic substance is found in water, this means the water is harmful to your health."

2. Have each student survey at least five adults, asking them if they have ever used nonhazardous substitutes for household cleaning. If so, ask them to share their ideas. If not, ask them why they chose not to use the substitutes. Write a paragraph about the survey results. Explain why most people choose not to use nonhazardous substitutes.

# Is Cleaning Hazardous to Your Health?

Your group will perform an investigation.  Here are the materials you will need:

- 3 Tbsp white vinegar
- 1 plastic cup and stirrer
- 1-2 shiny new pennies
- 1 Tbsp table salt
- 2-5 dirty, dull pennies
- commercial cleaning product (optional)

## Directions:

1. Add the table salt to the vinegar and stir.
2. Answer question 1.
3. Drop in your dirty, dull pennies
4. After five minutes, remove the pennies from the solution.
5. Answer questions 2-6 only.

## Questions:

1. Prediction:  What do you think will happen to the *pennies*? _____

   To the *liquid*? _____

   _____


2. Describe how your pennies look and feel when you take them out of the solution.

   Look? _____

   Feel? _____


3. Compare the treated pennies and the shiny pennies.  How are they alike and different?

   Alike? _____

   Different? _____


4. Think of a way to make the pennies look the same.  Try it!


5. Discuss the trade-offs of using the homemade cleaning solution versus a commercial product.


6. Mrs. Smith is a very busy person.  She has three children ages 2, 5, and 10, and also works 20 hours a week as a nurse.  She wants to keep her house very clean and also wants to take care of the environment.  Use the Decision Tree to help her decide if she would use 1. *a commercial product* containing toxic chemicals or 2. the *vinegar/salt solution* to remove tarnish from her nice silverware.

# Activity 6
## Further Explorations

1.  Find an area near your school where water seems to accumulate after a rain. Watch that area and make a map of the drainage pattern during the next rain.

2.  Visit the water treatment plant in your community or ask the manager to visit your class. Ask how water is treated. What price do residents pay? What chemicals are added to the water? What is the source of the water? Are there any particular problems with the water supply?

3.  Write a letter to a water conservation group (See *Resources* section) asking for information about what it is doing to help protect/conserve our water resources.

4.  Ask a county surveyor or city engineer for a drainage map of your area. Locate the school on the map. Trace a line on the map showing how water reaches your school from its source. Also show where runoff water and sewage go after leaving your school.

5.  Tour a factory in your area. Interview factory officials about water treatment in their factory. Is the water recycled? How is waste water treated? Where is it discharged? Are there any chemicals in the waste water? Are they safe or harmful? What kinds of EPA regulations must your factory follow?

6.  Research the Safe Drinking Water Act (SWDA) and the Clean Water Act. Write a report explaining how these laws have helped keep our water supplies safe.

7.  Contact your high school's or county's agricultural organization to find out what area farmers are doing to help keep pesticides and other chemicals out of water supplies.

8.  Write a story describing what life might be like on our planet in the future if we don't take proper care of our water supplies.

9.  Research the topic of wetlands. What are some ways they are helpful? What are some of the current controversies surrounding wetlands?

10. Working in teams, research what kind of chemicals and microorganisms occur naturally in water. Find out if they are dangerous if found in drinking water.

11. Wash your hair using rainwater. Record any differences.

12. Gather literature and other information on water softening systems. Investigate systems that do and do not use rock salt. What are the advantages and disadvantages of each?

# Activity 7
## Let's Talk It Over

**Teaching Suggestions:** Discuss the challenging (and sometimes controversial!) statements and questions below with your students. Help the students think critically by applying the concepts learned in this unit. Be prepared for some lively discussion!

1.  Our waterways frequently collect runoff from farmland that contains certain pesticides and other chemicals farmers use to grow and protect their crops. Should these chemicals be banned? Why or why not? What are the trade-offs in this situation?

2.  "Water from unpolluted, underground sources is completely pure." True or False? Discuss.

3.  "Factories should not be allowed to put <u>treated</u> wastewater back into streams and lakes." Do you agree or not? Why? Discuss.

4.  "Farmers should be able to decide if certain wetland areas on their own private land are used for agriculture or other purposes. The government has no right to tell them how to use their own property." Do you agree or disagree? Why?

5.  "Water containing small amounts of certain toxic chemicals is safe to drink. We shouldn't be worried about it." Do you agree? Why or why not? Discuss.

6.  "When homeowners and their families throw cleaning chemicals down the drain, they don't need to worry because their water treatment plant will remove the harmful chemicals before the water goes back into the community water source." Do you agree or disagree? Why?

7.  Fluoride and chlorine can be deadly to humans if swallowed in moderate quantities. Yet water companies routinely add these chemicals to our water! Should they be allowed to do this? Why or why not? Discuss.

8.  "The dose makes the poison." True or False? Explain.

9.  "It is important that we keep our water supply free of all chemical and organic pollutants, no matter what the cost." Do you agree or disagree with this statement? Explain why.

10. "Water supplies in the United States are basically *not* safe." Do you agree or disagree?

# Activity 8
## EEE Actions: You Can Make a Difference!

1. Develop a plan to reduce water consumption (and water bills!) in your home. Here are some possibilities to consider:

   a. Take short (5-7) minute showers. When taking a bath, don't fill the tub.

   b. Use faucets that have aerators that mix air and water.

   c. Don't let the water run continuously when brushing teeth or shaving.

   d. Scrape dishes well instead of rinsing them under running water.

   e. Use a nozzle that can be shut off when washing your car.

   f. Hose down cars, garbage cans, bicycles, etc., on the lawn, not the pavement.

   g. Clean off sidewalks with a broom, not a hose.

   h. Water plants during cool, windless hours, especially during early morning.

   i. Keep a jug of water in the refrigerator rather than running water from the tap until it gets cold enough to drink.

   j. Install devices that reduce the amount of water needed to flush toilets.

   k. While waiting for faucet water to get hot, catch the cool water in a pan and use it to cook or to water plants.

2. Encourage your classmates to develop good water conservation habits by organizing a "Water Drop" week. Students earn water drops by having an adult verify each time a gallon of water is saved at home or at school during the week. Students deposit their earned water drops into an empty aquarium located in a prominent place in the school. Students can solicit sponsors who will agree to donate $.05 for each gallon the student saves throughout the week. Sponsorship money can be used to set up a live display for all students to enjoy and be reminded of the life-supporting role water plays on our planet.

3. "Adopt" a stream in your community. Organize a clean-up group to pick up trash in and around the stream. Monitor the stream to make sure it stays clean.

4. Prepare an information exhibit featuring your "Clean the Stream" group and its project. Include pictures, poems, drawings, and a list of ways everyone can help, etc. Display the exhibit in your school, at a PTA meeting, or at a local shopping center.

5. Invite a guest speaker from your local Soil and Water Conservation Department to talk with your class about the proper use of land and water. Share the information you learned with students in the lower grades.

6. When practical, use nontoxic cleaning substances to clean your home.

# Activity 9
## The Case of the Off-Course Golf Course

**Student Directions:**

1. In this case study, you will examine a problem facing all communities – how to keep local lakes, streams, and rivers clean. While progress has been made in this area, work still needs to be done. In the scenario below, a fourth grade class tries to solve a pollution problem in their community. They discover that the solution is not simple.

2. Read and discuss the scenario below. Use the Decision Tree Worksheet to help your group come to a decision. Be prepared to defend your position.

---

### Scenario

Peter's teacher, Mr. Tilletzclean, is an environmentally sensitive person. He involved Peter's class in a project called "Save Our Streams." Each week the class took a water sample at three locations along a crooked creek which flows along the west side of town. The students noticed that there were many mayfly and stonefly nymphs in water samples taken from the northern section of the creek, but there were no mayfly and stonefly nymphs in samples taken further downstream. Instead, they found beetle larvae and dragonfly nymphs. Mr. Tilletzclean suggested studying the watershed map the class had drawn earlier. The students discovered that the Sparkling Brook Golf Course ran right along the creek near the south end of town.

It just so happened that Peter's dad was the golf pro at Sparkling Brook. That night Peter told his dad about what the class had discovered. His dad explained that some of the fertilizers, herbicides, and pesticides used to keep the grass healthy and looking nice must be running off into the small brook that flows through the property.

The next day, Peter reported this to the class. The class examined the watershed map and discovered that the small brook that ran through the golf course indeed emptied into the crooked creek. The students were quite upset. After further study it was confirmed that the runoff from the golf course was indeed changing the water in the creek just enough so that the mayfly and stonefly nymphs couldn't survive. "We must report our discovery to our local environmental groups. Maybe they can make the golf course stop using these chemicals!" exclaimed Sarah. "I agree," said Jim. "It's not fair that we all have to put up with polluted water just so some people can have fun playing golf! I don't even like watching it on TV."

My dad says that the golf course has to use lots of fertilizers on the greens and water them every day to keep them healthy and looking nice," explained Peter. "Also, without herbicides to kill weeds and pesticides to kill harmful insects, the fairway grass would not stay healthy. If we report this and the golf course has to stop using the chemicals, the grass and greens would get in a horrible condition. People would start going to

---

Salamander County to play golf. Our golf course would lose money and my dad would lose his job!"

"His dad's not the only one who'll be in trouble," said Sally. "My uncle owns the Hole in One Restaurant next to the golf course. He says business has never been better since the golf course opened. Maybe we could just get them to move the greens away from the brook. Then the fertilizers won't run off into the brook." Mr. Tilletzclean commented, "I've read about a new type of grass that is resistant to insects and stays green longer without much fertilization and water, but it's very expensive." Sally interrupted, "Remember when we talked about those ladybugs that ate aphids? Maybe the golf course could stop using pesticides and use insect predators instead."

Everybody seemed to have ideas about what do to. Someone even suggested that maybe it would be best to close down the course. Hopefully, Peter's dad could find another job. But then Joe remembered that the golf course always let the high school golf teams use the course free for practices. And since he was thinking of trying out for the golf team some day, well…

Mr. Tilletzclean finally helped the students narrow the argument down to two choices: 1. Don't report their findings, but continue to monitor the creek to make sure the condition doesn't get any worse, or 2. Report their findings and try to make the golf course stop using pesticides and fertilizer (even if it means large expenses for the golf course, possibly causing it to close.)

The students were definitely feeling like they were up a creek without a paddle! What should they do? Use your Decision tree and decide which way your group flows. Then answer the questions below.

1.    What is your group's decision?

      _____

2.    How would your decision affect the community?

      _____

      _____

3.    What is the **opportunity cost** of your choice?

      _____

4.    What are the **trade-offs** that are involved in this problem?

      _____

      _____

      _____

# Answers to Selected Teaching Activities

**Activity 4: Decision Time in Bonedry, California.** 1. a worsening scarcity of fresh water for the community caused by drought and irrigation needs. 2. yes. As the price rises, the Law of Demand says that people will purchase/use less. 3. Most – farmers, poorer people; Least – wealthier people. 4. Most – people who need large amounts of water and who would be willing to pay for it, farmers who were not rationed enough for their crops; Least – poorer people, people who don't use much water. 5. Answers will vary – see EEE Actions: You Can Make a Difference!

**Activity 5: Is Cleaning Hazardous to Your Health?** 2. The pennies will lose the tarnish, but will remain dull. There will not be much difference in smoothness. 3. Pennies from the solution are not as shiny as new pennies, but both have no tarnish. 4. Rub the pennies to give them some shine. 5. giving up some cleaning ability and time in order to provide some environmental benefits.

**Activity 9: Decision Tree Model:**

*Choice 1: Don't Report Findings, but Monitor:* <u>Good Points:</u> Golf course doesn't close down, restaurant stays open, stream doesn't get worse, people keep jobs. <u>Bad Points:</u> Stream stays "polluted."

*Choice 2: Report Findings, with Suggestions:* <u>Good Points:</u> Pollution reduced. <u>Bad Points:</u> high costs for golf course, possible loss of jobs, possible shut-down.

**Five Step Model:**

| Decision-Making Grid Answer Key<br>The Off-Course Golf Course | | | |
|---|---|---|---|
| **Criteria** | | | |
| **Alternatives** | **Effect on Environment** | **Effect on Jobs** | **Effect on Businesses** |
| Don't Report Findings - Monitor | - | + | + |
| Report Findings - Stop Fertilizer and Pesticides | + | - or ? | - |

**Important Note:** *Notice that students cannot simply count the good and bad points.* Their final decision will hinge on how they *weigh/value* the criteria (their good and bad points.)

3. The opportunity cost is the value/benefit of the choice they *don't* select.

4. The main trade-off is environmental quality versus jobs and economic growth.

# Unit 4

# Energy Resources

# Overview of Unit 4

## Energy Resources

### Introduction:

There has been a renewed interest recently in the topic of energy. One reason has been the increase in the price of oil and natural gas and the perceived vulnerability of the United States to an increasing dependence on foreign energy supplies. Higher energy prices have also renewed interest in non-fossil fuel sources of energy, such as wind, solar, and nuclear power. What are the advantages and disadvantages of different sources of energy? Will we run out of energy? Do fossil fuels damage the environment? Is it wise to maximize one's energy efficiency? Your students will enjoy studying the answers to these and other interesting questions.

### Learning Objectives:

After completing this unit students will be able to:

1. Identify advantages and disadvantages of different energy sources.

2. Apply different economic concepts to energy issues.

3. Explain various ways to conserve energy.

### Unit Outline:

I. Facts About Energy Resources

II. Teaching Instructions and Key Concepts to Emphasize

III. Specific Teaching Activities

1. Sources of Energy
2. Production of Electricity
3. Energy Search
4. Energy Efficiency
5. Further Explorations
6. Let's Talk It Over
7. EEE Actions – You Can Make a Difference!
8. Case Study - The Case of the Outdoor Lab

IV. Answers to Selected Teaching Activities

# Facts About Energy Resources

## Energy Basics

MEASURING ENERGY: **Energy** can be defined as the capacity to do work. The unit of measurement used to express the heat contained in energy resources is called a **British thermal unit** or **Btu.** One Btu is the heat energy needed to raise the temperature of one pound of water one degree Fahrenheit. A Btu is quite small. For example, if allowed to burn completely, a wooden kitchen match gives off one Btu of energy. A quad is used to measure very large amounts of energy. A **quad** is equal to one quadrillion (1,000,000,000,000,000) Btu's. The United States uses an enormous amount of energy – about one quad of energy every 3.9 days!

ENERGY SOURCES: There are many **primary energy sources** used in the United States, including petroleum, coal, natural gas, nuclear, hydropower, propane, geothermal, wind, solar, and biomass. Figure 4-1 shows the breakdown by energy source.

Figure 4-1

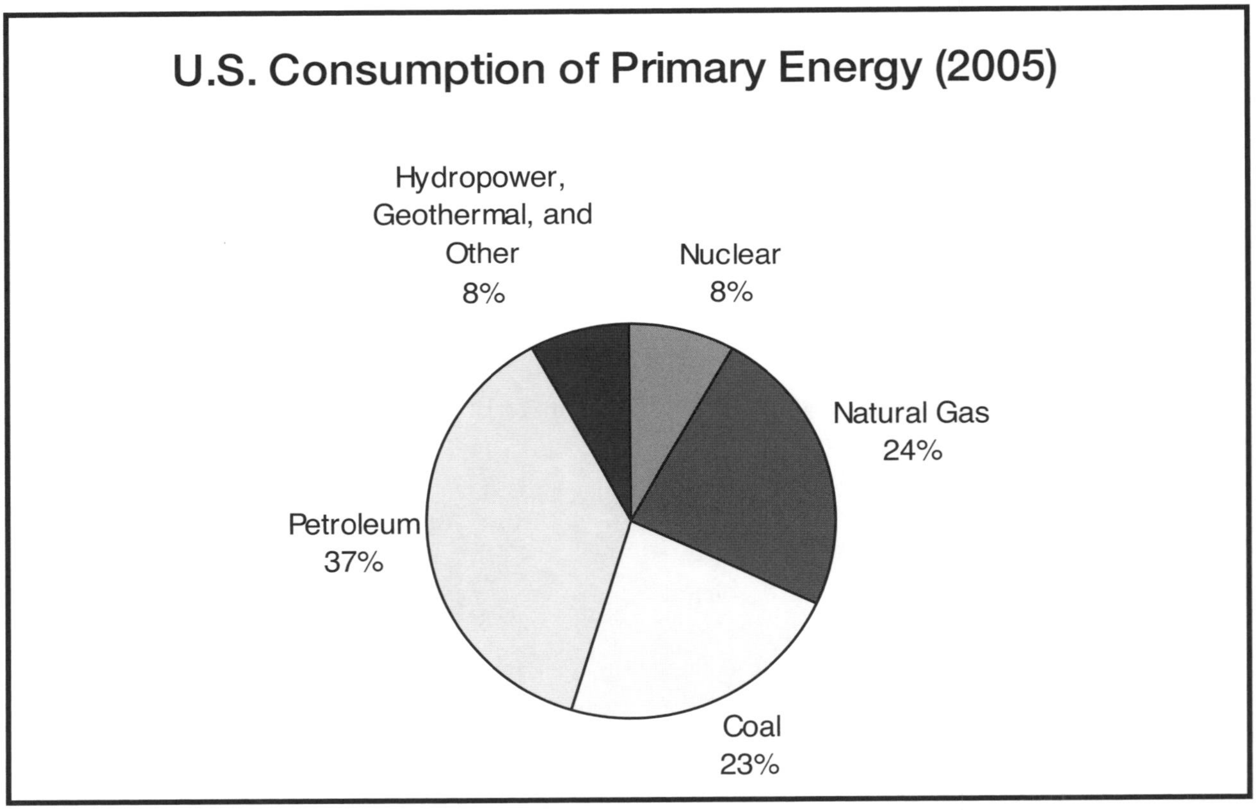

## U.S. Consumption of Primary Energy (2005)

Hydropower, Geothermal, and Other
8%

Nuclear
8%

Natural Gas
24%

Petroleum
37%

Coal
23%

These primary energy sources are classified as renewable or nonrenewable. **Renewable energy** sources are those that can be replenished quickly or that are nondepletable. Examples include solar, hydropower, wind, geothermal, and biomass. **Nonrenewable energy** sources are finite. Examples are nuclear energy and fossil fuels, such as coal, petroleum, and natural gas.

ELECTRICITY: Electricity is a **secondary energy source**, which means that we must use primary sources to produce it. According to the Energy Information Administration of the U.S. Department of Energy, "more than one-third of the primary energy in the nation is used to generate electricity" (www.eia.doe.gov/cneaf/electricity/page/prim2/chapter2.html). Coal, nuclear, hydropower, natural gas, and petroleum are the top five primary sources for producing electricity, with coal (more than one-half) as the largest source (www.eia.doe.gov/kids/energyfacts/sources/nonrenewable/coal.html). Unlike the primary energy sources, electricity is not classified as renewable or nonrenewable.

TRENDS IN UNITED STATES ENERGY CONSUMPTION: As the economy and population of the United States have grown, so has energy consumption. However, this increase has been marked by remarkable increases in **energy efficiency**. For example, in 2002, the United States consumed about 25-30 percent more energy than annually during the 1970s, while the population grew by 30 percent. However, the value of the nation's real **Gross Domestic Product (GDP** - the total value of all the final goods and services produced in the economy in a year) was 80 percent higher! The United States has improved its energy/GDP ratio as fast or faster than other developed countries. This improvement in energy efficiency was partially a response to the rapid increases in crude oil prices in the 1970s.

# Renewable Energy Sources

RECENT TRENDS: In the 1970s, the federal government's renewable energy program grew rapidly to include not only basic and applied **research and development (R & D)**, but also participation in private sector initiatives. In the 1980s, this interest waned as the price of oil fell. In constant dollar (real) terms, government spending for R & D in renewable energy declined 90 percent, from a peak of $875 million in 1979, to a low of $84 million in 1990. In 1990, this trend was reversed. Constant dollar R & D spending in 1992 was $146 million, which rose to $111 billion by 1999. This dramatic funding increase reflects fear of environmental damage, especially acid rain and global warming, from burning fossil fuels.

To what extent the United States continues to subsidize the development of renewable energy will be a subject of much future debate.

RENEWABLE ENERGY SOURCES: The following information presents basic facts about four renewable energy sources and lists some advantages and disadvantages of each.

_Solar Energy_: **Solar energy** is produced in the core of the sun. In a process called **nuclear fusion**, the intense heat in the sun causes hydrogen atoms to break apart and fuse together to form helium atoms. A very small amount of mass is lost in this process. This lost matter is emitted into space as radiant energy. Less than one percent of this energy reaches the earth, yet it is enough to provide all of the earth's energy needs. The sun's energy travels at the speed of light (186,000 miles per second) and reaches the earth in about eight minutes. Capturing the sun's energy is not easy since solar energy is spread out over such a large area. The energy a specific land area receives depends on various factors such as time of day, season of the year, cloudiness of the sky, and proximity to the equator.

One primary use of solar energy is **home heating**. There are two basic kinds of solar heating systems: active and passive. In an **active system**, special equipment (such as a solar collector) is used to collect and distribute the solar energy. In a **passive system**, the home is designed to let in large amounts of sunlight. The heat produced from the light is trapped inside. A passive system does not rely on special mechanical equipment.

Another primary use of solar energy is **producing electricity**. The most familiar way is using **photovoltaic (PV) cells**, which are used to power toys, calculators, and roadside telephone call boxes. Photovoltaics is a process that directly converts solar energy to electricity. It has become more affordable due to private research. In 1976, the average market price for a photovoltaic module was $44 per peak watt installed, but by 2000 this had fallen to $3.46 per peak watt. The other primary way to produce electricity is using **solar thermal systems.** Large collectors concentrate the sunlight onto a receiver to superheat a liquid, which is used to make steam to power electrical generators.

| Advantages of Solar Energy | Disadvantages of Solar Energy |
|---|---|
| * Unlimited supply<br>* No air or water pollution | * May not be cost effective<br>* Storage and backup are necessary<br>* Reliability depends on availability of sunlight<br>* Land intensive |

*Hydropower*: **Hydropower** is energy that comes from the force of moving water. Hydropower is a renewable energy source because it is replenished constantly by the fall and flow of snow and rainfall in the **water cycle.** As water flows through devices, such as a water wheel or turbine of a dam, the **kinetic** (motion) **energy** of water is converted to **mechanical energy**, which can be used to grind grain, drive a sawmill, pump water, or produce electricity.

The primary way hydropower is used today in the United States is to produce electricity. In 2003, hydropower provided 7.0 percent of the nation's electricity. Although a hydroelectric power plant is initially expensive to build, in the long run it is the cheapest way to produce electricity, primarily because the energy source, moving water, is free. Recently, many people have built smaller hydroelectric systems that produce enough electricity to power a few homes.

| Advantages of Hydropower | Disadvantages of Hydropower |
|---|---|
| * Abundant, clean, and safe<br>* Easily stored in reservoirs<br>* Relatively inexpensive way to produce electricity in the long run<br>* Recreational benefits like boating, fishing, etc. | * Significant environmental impact<br>* Water supply is needed<br>* Best sites for dams already developed |

_Wind Energy_:  **Wind** is air in motion.  It is caused by the uneven heating of the earth's surface by the sun.  Wind power has been used for thousands of years to convert the wind's kinetic (motion) energy into mechanical energy for grinding grain or pumping water.  Today, wind machines are used increasingly to produce electricity.

The two most common types of wind machines used for producing electricity are horizontal and vertical.  **Horizontal machines** have blades that look like airplane propellers.  **Vertical machines** look like giant egg-beaters.  The vertical machines are easier to maintain, can accept wind from any direction, and don't require protective features to guard against high winds.  However, horizontal machines produce _more_ electricity, and for this reason are used more often than their vertical counterparts.

Most electricity production occurs on large **wind farms**.  The majority of  wind farms are owned by independent producers who operate the farms and sell electricity to utility companies for distribution.  The **Public Utility Regulatory Policies Act (PURPA)** requires utility companies to purchase electricity from independent energy producers at fair and nondiscriminatory rates.  In 2003, wind energy provided the United States with less than 1.0 percent of its total electricity.  California currently produces twice as much as any other state.  Many predict that wind energy will provide much more of our future electrical production.

| Advantages of Wind Energy | Disadvantages of Wind Energy |
| --- | --- |
| * A "free" source of energy<br>* No water or air pollution<br>* Wind farms are relatively inexpensive to build | * Requires constant and significant amounts of wind<br>* Wind farms require large tracts of land<br>* Can have a negative visual impact on landscapes<br>* Risk to endangered birds of prey |

_Biomass_:  **Biomass** is any organic substance that can be used as an energy source.  The most common examples are wood, crops, seaweed, and animal waste.  Biomass has been used for thousands of years and is the oldest known energy source.  It is a renewable energy source because its supply is unlimited – more can always be produced in a relatively short time.

All biomass is converted solar energy.  The energy is stored in biomass through the process of **photosynthesis**, in which plants combine carbon dioxide, water, and certain minerals to form carbohydrates.  The most common way to release the energy from biomass is burning.  Other ways are bacterial decay, fermentation, and conversion.

There are four main types of biomass: (1) wood and agricultural products, (2) solid waste, (3) landfill gas, and (4) alcohol fuels. Wood is by far the most common form, accounting for about 70 percent of all biomass energy. Burning solid waste is a common practice, and people have done it for thousands of years. What is new is burning waste to produce electricity. **Waste-to-energy** power plants operate like a traditional coal plant, except garbage is used to produce steam to run the turbines. Although it typically costs more to produce electricity using biomass, the great advantage is that it reduces the amount of waste entering landfills. Some people have environmental concerns about waste-to-energy plants, but because it is becoming increasingly difficult to determine sites for landfills, these plants are an increasingly attractive option.

The **methane** produced in landfills by the decay of organic matter is another source of biomass energy. A landfill owner in Indianapolis uses the methane to heat his greenhouse, thus reducing the operating costs of his on-site nursery business.

Corn, wheat, and other crops can be used to produce a variety of liquid fuels. The most common are ethanol and methanol. Today these are relatively high-cost fuels, and the price of oil must continue to rise to make them a cost-effective option. However, a mixture of 10 percent ethanol and 90 percent gasoline produces a fuel called **gasohol**. Gasohol is more cost competitive and can be used in a traditional gasoline engine. It also has a higher octane rating than gasoline and is cleaner burning.

| Advantages of Biomass | Disadvantages of Biomass |
|---|---|
| * Abundant and renewable<br>* Way to dispose of solid waste | * Air pollution from burning biomass<br>* May not be cost effective |

# Nonrenewable Energy Sources

RECENT TRENDS: The United States depends very heavily on nonrenewable energy sources. Coal, natural gas, petroleum, and nuclear energy together accounted for close to 95 percent of the energy consumed in the United States in 2005. The three fossil fuels accounted for over 89 percent of that amount. The main reason the use of renewable energy has not increased significantly is that nonrenewable energy sources are abundant and relatively inexpensive. This pattern will continue in the foreseeable future as new technologies make nonrenewable energy exploration and production more efficient.

NONRENEWABLE ENERGY SOURCES: The following information presents basic facts about four nonrenewable energy sources and lists some advantages and disadvantages of each of them.

<u>Coal</u>:  Coal is our most abundant fossil fuel.  We have more coal reserves than any other nation, enough to last over 300 years at today's rate of use.  Coal is used to make close to 50 percent of the electricity produced in the United States, with electric power plants using over 85 percent of all the coal used.

There are three major types of coal:  lignite, bituminous, and anthracite.  They are classified by hardness, with lignite being the least hard and anthracite the hardest.  The harder the coal, the more efficient it is as a heat source.  There are two basic ways to mine coal:  **surface (strip) mining** and **underground mining**.  Surface mining is used when coal is found close to the surface.  It is used to mine over 50 percent of the coal in the United States.  Underground mining is used to extract coal lying deep beneath the surface.  It is more dangerous than surface mining, so there are many regulations to ensure worker safety.

The two biggest environmental concerns with coal are the effects of **mining** and **air pollution**.  Although coal mining does alter the landscape, federal law now requires mined land to be restored to a land use classification that is equal to or better than its original condition.  A company must file an extensive reclamation plan before any mining can take place.

The biggest air pollution concern is with the two byproducts of coal combustion:  **sulfur dioxide gas** and **ash particles**.  When mixed with other chemicals, sulfur dioxide can be a health hazard.  Also, sulfur dioxide combines with nitrogen compounds to form acid rain, which can damage lakes, forests, and streams.  To reduce emissions, companies clean coal before it is burned, increase combustion efficiencies, burn higher grade coal, and remove pollutants (often with **scrubbers**) after the coal is burned.  Ash particles fly into the air when coal burns, so companies use special devices to trap the particles in the stack.

Burning coal also releases carbon dioxide, a "greenhouse" gas. Many scientist believe that increases in greenhouse emissions contribute to global warming. (See Unit 4 for a discussion of this controversial issue.)

| Advantages of Coal | Disadvantages of Coal |
|---|---|
| * Abundant and cheap<br>* United States has large supplies<br>* A "compact" heat source | * Considered a "dirty" fuel<br>* Can have negative impact on environment<br>* Burning releases carbon dioxide, with a potential effect on global warming |

<u>Petroleum</u>:  The United States consumes more petroleum (37.2 percent) than any other source of energy, which is 25 percent of the world's petroleum consumption.  The three biggest sector users of petroleum in 2004 were transportation (68 percent), industry (24 percent), and home and businesses (8 percent).  About 6,000 products are made from petroleum.  To be made into gasoline, petroleum is **refined**.  Refining removes unnecessary sulfur from oil, which increases gasoline efficiency and reduces pollution.

The largest oil producer in the world in 2004 was Saudi Arabia, followed by Russia, the United States, Iran, and Mexico. The former Soviet Union used to be the largest producer, but political upheaval hampered production. In 2004, net imports to the U.S. of petroleum equaled 58 percent, up from 41 percent in 1992 and 30 percent in 1985. The OPEC nations are major suppliers, the leading nation being Saudi Arabia. The U.S. currently imports 57 percent of the oil we consume, projected to grow to 70 percent by 2025. Of all the oil we consume, 45 percent goes into gasoline, the rest into aviation fuel, diesel fuel, home heating oil, and petrochemicals.

Oil is found using **seismic technology**. Special instruments, called **seismographs**, record reflected sound waves created by explosives. These waves give a rough picture of the geological formations and rock layers, providing clues about possible oil deposits. Exploring for oil is very risky, with 19 out of 20 wells turning up dry. For this reason, low oil prices, while beneficial for the average consumer, discourage exploration and production.

Oil shale is sedimentary rock containing an oil-like compound. The United States has substantial oil shale reserves; however, the current price of oil would have to rise to make shale oil recovery competitive with other sources of energy.

| Advantages of Petroleum | Disadvantages |
|---|---|
| * Abundant<br>* Easy to use<br>* Relatively cheap | * Contributes to pollution<br>* United States must import over 50 percent of supply<br>* Price can fluctuate greatly because of OPEC control of large oil supplies |

_Natural Gas_: Natural gas is a colorless, odorless gas composed mainly of methane, a natural compound formed when plant and animal matter decays. Natural gas is found trapped underground in porous rocks and is reached by drilling. Companies add an odorant to give natural gas its characteristic smell.

In the last 25 years, the use of natural gas in the United States has grown significantly, and currently accounts for almost 25 percent of total primary energy consumption. In 2002, U.S. net imports accounted for 15 percent of natural gas use. The United States produces about 85 percent of its natural gas, which is nearly 25 percent of the world's total production. Experts estimate that, at current rates of consumption, the United States has at least a 50 year supply.

Industry is the largest consumer of natural gas, which is used primarily to fuel boilers in manufacturing. The residential sector is the second largest user. About seven out of ten homes in the United States are warmed with natural gas. Electric utility companies also use much natural gas. After coal and nuclear energy, natural gas is the third leading fuel for electricity production. A major advantage of natural gas as a primary energy source is that it is relatively safe for the environment. It is cleaner burning than coal and petroleum and emits no sulfur dioxide or ash particles. Natural gas can also be used for transportation. It is clean burning, is safe to use, and has a reasonable cost. Natural gas is transported primarily by pipeline. It can be converted into a liquid and then transported by ship throughout the world.

When consumers pay their gas bills, they are paying for exploration, drilling, leasing of land, operating costs, depreciation, return on investment, and taxes. In fact, Federal and State taxes make up approximately 27 percent of the retail gas price. Local gas taxes may also add to the price of gas.

| Advantages of Natural Gas | Disadvantages of Natural Gas |
|---|---|
| * Abundant supply<br>* Relatively inexpensive<br>* Clean burning – low pollution | * Difficult to store and transport in gas form<br>* Drilling/Exploration is expensive and time consuming |

*Nuclear Energy*: The basic substance used to produce nuclear energy is **uranium**, an abundant, nonrenewable resource. A ton of uranium ore in the United States typically contains three to four pounds of uranium. In this country, uranium is produced mainly in New Mexico and Wyoming. But because most mines in the U.S. have closed, about 75 percent of refined uranium used domestically each year is imported, with Canada being the largest single supplier. At current rates of consumption, uranium reserves are estimated to last over 500 years.

Uranium is not burned to produce energy. Instead, large amounts of energy are released when the tiny uranium atoms are split. In size, an atom of uranium compares to an apple, as an apple compares to the earth.

About eight percent of total United States primary energy consumption comes from nuclear energy, which is used almost entirely to produce electricity. In 2005, nuclear energy generated over 20 percent of the electricity in the United States. France, Belgium, and the Republic of Korea rely on nuclear energy for more than 50 percent of their electricity.

In the United States, all nuclear power plants must obtain a permit to begin construction and later must obtain a license to begin operations. The Nuclear Regulatory Commission is the agency responsible for licensing. Obtaining a new license is a lengthy process, and local hearings are held so that residents can express their opinions. The average time needed to complete the construction of a nuclear plant and put it into operation in the United States is 14 years. The lengthy licensing procedure, coupled with environmental, safety, and economic concerns, has contributed to the decline in the number of planned nuclear plants. Since 1977, no orders for new plants have been announced.

| Advantages of Nuclear Energy | Disadvantages of Nuclear Energy |
|---|---|
| * Uranium is abundant and inexpensive<br>* Reduces dependence on foreign oil<br>* No air pollution, since fuel is<br>   not burned | * Potential dangers of exposure to radiation<br>* No set method for disposing of<br>   radioactive wastes<br>* High initial construction, finance, and<br>   licensing costs |

ENERGY EFFICIENCY VERSUS ECONOMIC EFFICIENCY:  Economists are concerned with the overall **economic efficiency** of the economic system.  This means getting the greatest benefit from <u>all</u> of our **scarce** productive resources.  **Energy efficiency**, a narrower concept, means getting the greatest benefit from our <u>energy</u> resources.  Sometimes these goals conflict. For example, we could make automobiles today that average more than 100 miles per gallon. This would result in better **energy conservation**, but would we be willing to pay the cost in terms of lack of power, crash protection, and load capacity?

THE ROLE OF PRICE IN GUIDING DECISIONS ABOUT ENERGY:  In market economies, resource allocation is guided primarily by market prices.  These prices help society determine answers to the crucial questions of what, how, and for whom to produce.  However, in the area of energy policy, many advocate significant levels of government intervention in energy markets.  The intervention often takes the form of **subsidies** for the development of alternative energy sources which currently may not be cost effective.

From 1995-2005, the **market price** of oil ranged from $22-$50 per barrel.  These prices are high enough for oil producers to make a profit while allowing consumers to enjoy the many benefits of this valuable source of energy. With colder winters and warmer summers, several devastating hurricanes, and the Iraq War, oil prices sparked higher gasoline prices during 2004-2005, which have since moderately declined.  Oil remains an abundant source of energy. *Should the government subsidize more expensive forms of renewable energy, given the current price of oil (and other fossil fuels)?*

Proponents contend that subsidies are necessary to help reduce our dependence on finite fossil fuels.  Proponents also point out that relying more on renewable energy will reduce our dependence on foreign oil suppliers and will result in less pollution of the environment.

Subsidy opponents argue that we will never "run out" of fossil fuels. As fossil fuels become scarcer, their market price will rise, encouraging consumers to use less. The higher price also will make it profitable for energy companies to invest in new fossil fuel production technologies and to invest in alternative energy sources, including renewable energy. This simultaneous *decrease* in the quantity of energy demanded and *increase* in the quantity of energy supplied occurs automatically, without costly and inefficient government intervention. Opponents of subsidies agree with subsidy proponents that the environmental costs of fossil fuels should be reflected in their price, and that this should be an important consideration when dealing with this issue. Opponents contend that the best way to lessen the danger of a cut-off in foreign supplies is to build a **strategic petroleum reserve.**

The issue of the development of alternative energy sources is a complicated one. The key point to remember is that there is an **opportunity cost** to every economic decision. Using tax revenues to subsidize alternative energy means giving up some other valuable use for those revenues. In energy policy, as in all public policy, decision makers must consider all the opportunity costs when determining **trade-offs** among different policy goals.

# Teaching Activities

# Teaching Instructions

## Overview:

As in the other units, you will probably want to do the Case Study toward the end of the unit when students have mastered much of the basic information. Some of the basic information to teach your students is found in the preceding *Facts About Energy Resources* section. Other information is available from a variety of resources, many of which are listed in the *Resources* section. An especially valuable resource is the National Energy Education Development (NEED) Project. See www.need.org.

## Important Concepts To Emphasize:

1. **There Are No Free Sources of Energy:** It takes scarce productive resources to provide every type of energy, even "free" sources, such as wind and solar power.

2. **There are Advantages and Disadvantages to Each Energy Source:** Each source of energy has certain advantages and disadvantages. This makes the choice of which energy source to use difficult and sometimes controversial.

3. **Energy Conservation Means More Than Just Not Using Our Energy Resources:** One way of conserving energy resources is by using them efficiently. For example, we want to conserve oil so that we get the maximum benefit from our finite supplies. We could "conserve" oil by never using it, but that would mean giving up all the valuable uses that oil provides. We should manage our scarce energy (and other natural resources) to provide the greatest net benefit to present and future generations combined after considering all of the costs and benefits involved, including the environmental costs.

4. **The Price of an Energy Resource Reflects its Relative Scarcity:** Energy resources, which are relatively more scarce cost more than those which are relatively less scarce.

5. **We Will Never Run Out of Oil or Any Other Nonrenewable Resources:** This doesn't mean we can use energy sources without thought for tomorrow. Rather, it means that as an energy source becomes increasingly scarce, its market price will rise, discouraging consumption and encouraging production of alternative energy sources. For example, during the 19th century, whalers nearly drove some species of whales to extinction. As this happened, the market price of whales and whale products inevitably rose. Whale oil became so expensive that petroleum became commercially feasible and whale oil lamps were phased out in favor of cheaper kerosene. The survival of the whales was aided by the free market response to their increasing scarcity. The same dynamics will take place in oil markets. As oil becomes increasingly scarce, its market price will rise, discouraging consumption, and encouraging the development of other energy sources.

# Activity 1
## Sources of Energy

---

**Teaching Objective:**  After completing this activity, students will be able to:

1.  Identify two groups of energy resources.
2.  Identify the advantages and disadvantages of various energy sources.
3.  Explain why energy resources are considered scarce.
4.  Explain that informed energy decisions require an understanding of specific energy resources, and that when a choice is made to use a particular energy resource, there are always trade-offs.

**Time Allowed:**  Two 30-minute sessions

**Materials:**
- Resources (textbooks, pamphlets, etc.) on energy resources
- Energy Facts Cards (make with index cards)
- Decision Tree or Five-Step Model worksheets (pgs. 18-20)
- Energy Resources Worksheet

**Vocabulary/Concepts:**

- *Energy*:  the capacity to do work

- *Energy Efficiency*:  the amount of useful energy you get from a system

- *British Thermal Unit*:  The heat energy needed to raise the temperature of one pound of water one degree Fahrenheit

- *Nonrenewable Energy*:  energy resources such as fossil fuels that are limited in supply

- *Hydropower*:  energy that comes from the force of moving water

- *Fossil Fuels*:  fuels such as petroleum, coal, and natural gas which are formed by the compacting of decayed animal and plant materials

- *Wind Energy*:  energy that comes from the movement of air

- *Nuclear Energy*:  energy from the nucleus of an atom that is released through fission

- *Solar Energy*:  energy that comes from the sun

- *Price*:  Price is the amount people pay to buy a good, service, or productive resource.  Price is a reflection of how scarce something is relative to other things.

- *Trade-Offs*:  giving up some of one thing in order to get more of another

Energy resources are *scarce* resources – they are not freely available in unlimited quantities. Energy is required in all production and consumption. Producing energy requires scarce **productive resources** (natural, human, and capital). The **price** of an energy resource reflects its relative scarcity. Resources which are more scarce generally cost more than resources which are less scarce. The different energy resources have distinct advantages and disadvantages which must be considered when deciding which energy source to use in a particular situation.

## Teaching Procedure:

Introduce Vocabulary and Basic Concepts

1.　　Write the word "Energy" on the board or overhead. Ask students to identify different **primary energy sources**. Briefly discuss these primary energy sources as you write them on the board. Write them on the board according to the pattern on the web/concept map below. You can add picture clues as you go along. <u>Do not write the words Renewable, Nonrenewable, or Fossil Fuels.</u>

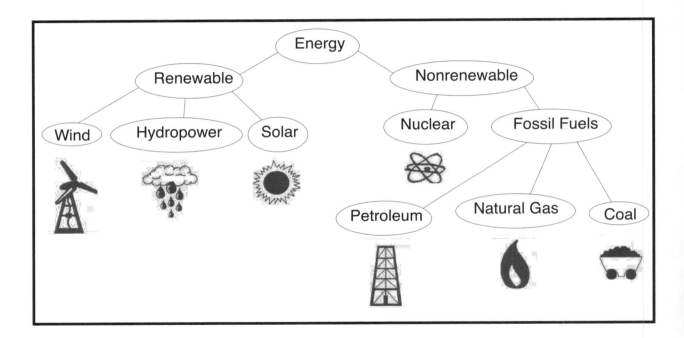

2.　　Ask students if they can explain how you grouped the energy sources. Is there a pattern? Explain the concepts of **renewable** and **nonrenewable** energy sources and **fossil fuels**.

3.　　Ask students which energy source they think is "best." Discuss student responses. Explain the need "to know more" in order to decide what energy source to use. Explain that students will form research teams to find out more about each energy source.

Procedure

1.  Divide the class into cooperative groups of seven. Once in their groups, assign each student to an "expert group," either coal, nuclear, solar, petroleum, natural gas, wind, or hydropower. Tell students that they will gather information in their expert group and report back to their original cooperative group.

2.  Give each expert group a file of information and websites about a specific energy source. This information can come from student textbooks, encyclopedias, and other sources. (See EEE *Resources* section.) Students can also use the Energy Fact Cards, which summarize basic energy information.

3.  After a period of time, student "experts" report back to their original group to share information. After each expert reports, each student should complete an Energy Resource Worksheet on the advantages and disadvantages of each energy source.

4.  The teacher should review the information with the entire class. A transparency of the worksheet may be helpful. Elaborate on the advantages and disadvantages of the different energy sources. In your discussion, explain/review the economic concepts of **scarcity, price,** and **trade-offs**. Use the questions in the Key Questions to Ask Students below.

<u>Follow-up Activity with the Decision Tree or Five-Step Model</u>

1.  Review how to use the Decision Tree or Five-Step Models.

2.  Divide the class into *new* groups of three or four students. Give each group <u>two</u> Energy Facts Cards. Using these and their own notes, have the group discuss which of these two energy sources they would choose for their own community. Students should fill in a Decision Tree or Five-Step Model decision grid.

3.  Share group decisions with the rest of the class.

## Key Questions To Ask Students:

1.  Why is energy considered scarce? *(It is not freely available in unlimited quantities. It takes scarce productive resources to produce energy. Energy, therefore, has a price, and both producers and consumers must pay to get it.)*

2.  What does the price of a good, service, or resource tell us? *(The price tells us how scarce an item is relative to other items.)*

3.  What are the things (criteria) one must consider when trying to choose the best energy source? *(price/cost, pollution effects, environmental impact, reliability, safety, availability, aesthetic effects, etc.)*

4.  Which criteria in question 3 are most important? *(It depends on the situation and the particular values of those making the decision.)*

5.    What does trade-off mean?  *(when making a choice, giving up some of one thing to get some of another)*

6.    Suppose your state built a coal power plant instead of a solar power plant.  What would be some of the trade-offs?  *(giving up some environmental benefits, but gaining an abundant, reliable, and relatively cheap source of energy.)*

## Bulletin Board Ideas:

1.    Create a collage of the word/web concept map that was discussed in class.  Add a picture and have a card listing advantages and disadvantages next to each energy source.

2.    Make an "Energy in the News" display using newspaper and magazine articles.  Highlight basic facts and main ideas.  Later, assign students to this task.

3.    Divide students into groups and assign each group an energy source.  Students must create a "persuasive" poster to encourage usage of their energy source, stressing the advantages.

## Student Journal Ideas:

1.    Write a paragraph/story about the "perfect" energy source.  What would it be like?  Why would it be better than the current sources?  Give a name to this new source.

2.    Describe energy use in the "Society of the Future."

3.    Write a paragraph explaining the importance of being informed of both the advantages and disadvantages of various energy sources.

# ENERGY FACTS CARDS

## Solar Energy

**Advantages**

Unlimited supply
No air pollution
No water pollution

**Disadvantages**

Storage needed
Backup energy source needed
Reliability depends on sunlight
Can be very costly to produce
Very land intensive

## Hydropower

**Advantages**

Easily stored in reservoirs that help control flooding
Fairly inexpensive
Offers water recreation
Abundant, clean, and safe
Hydro plants are energy efficient- the cheapest
    energy source

**Disadvantages**

Requires a water supply
Dams and reservoirs can disrupt
    environment
Best sites already developed

## Wind

**Advantages**

No air or water pollution
Fairly inexpensive to build
Cost of producing electricity from wind
    is dropping
"Free" source of energy
Land around wind farms can be
    used for other purposes

**Disadvantages**

Needs constant and large amounts
    of wind
Requires large amounts of land
Some wind farms cause
    "noise pollution"
Negative visual effect on the landscape
Can harm bird populations

# Natural Gas

## Advantages

United States has abundant supply
Relatively inexpensive
Cleanburning - not much pollution

## Disadvantages

Difficult to store and transport in
    gas form
Drilling and exploration is expensive
    and time consuming
Releases carbon dioxide when burned

# Petroleum

## Advantages

Abundant source worldwide
Easy to use
Relatively cheap
Used to produce many products

## Disadvantages

Contributes to air pollution
Must import about 60% of our supply
Price can change suddenly because of
    OPEC control
Burning releases carbon dioxide

# Nuclear (Uranium)

## Advantages

No air pollution
Fuel costs are low
Abundant uranium supplies

## Disadvantages

Plants costly to build because of many
    safety regulations
Thermal pollution
Public concern for safety
Must determine how to dispose of
    radioactive waste

# Coal

## Advantages

Our most abundant fossil fuel
More compact heat source than wood
A low cost fuel

## Disadvantages

Air pollution/acid rain concerns
Possible negative visual effects on
    environment – strip mining
Hazards of coal mining
Releases carbon dioxide when burned

# Energy Resources Worksheet

## Renewable Energy Resources:

**Solar**    Advantages _____

_____

Disadvantages _____

_____

**Wind**    Advantages _____

_____

Disadvantages _____

_____

**Hydropower**    Advantages _____

_____

Disadvantages _____

_____

## Nonrenewable Energy Resources

**Nuclear**    Advantages _____

_____

Disadvantages _____

_____

**Coal**    Advantages _____

_____

Disadvantages _____

_____

**Petroleum**    Advantages _____

_____

Disadvantages _____

_____

**Natural Gas**    Advantages _____

_____

Disadvantages _____

_____

# Activity 2
## Production of Energy

**Teaching Objectives:** After completing this activity, students will be able to:

1. Explain the importance of energy in both production and consumption.
2. Identify nonrenewable and renewable energy sources as primary energy sources and electricity as a secondary energy source.
3. Explain the process of electricity generation.
4. Explain what factors influence the energy source that will be used in a certain state or region.

**Time Allowed:** Two 30-minute sessions
1. Introduction and Electricity Generation
2. Map Exercise

**Materials:** • Copies of U.S. map and Energy Sources Information Sheet

**Vocabulary/Concepts:**

- *Consumers:* buyers and users of goods and services

- *Imports:* goods or services purchased from other countries

- *Primary Energy Sources:* direct energy sources, such as coal, oil, uranium, natural gas, or wind

- *Producers:* those who use productive resources to make goods and services

- *Productive Resources:* the inputs (natural, human, and capital) needed to produce goods and services

- *Secondary Energy Source:* an energy source, such as electricity, that is produced using a direct energy source

All **producers** and **consumers** use energy. Energy sources that are used directly (such as coal, oil, uranium, natural gas, wind, etc.) are called **primary energy sources.** Energy sources, such as electricity, which are produced from primary energy, are called **secondary energy sources.** Since it takes scarce **productive resources** to produce energy, energy is not freely available in unlimited quantities. Thus, energy is considered a **scarce** resource, and both consumers and producers must pay to obtain it. The type of energy used in a state or region depends on several factors, including the market price of energy resources, regional availability, government regulations, and political factors.

# Teaching Procedure:

Introduction to Electricity Generation

1.  Construct a word web/concept map on energy using the blackboard or chart paper. Initiate the discussion with this statement: "Energy exists in every produced item." Have students look around the room to name items which use energy or were produced by the use of energy. Group items around categories of lighting, heating/cooling, machines (clock or computer), and the manufacture of goods (desk, chair).

2.  Explain the difference between a **primary source** of energy (coal, uranium, oil, wind, etc.) and a **secondary source** (electricity). Discuss whether energy should be considered **scarce.** (*Yes, it takes scarce productive resources to produce. It is not freely available in unlimited quantities. One must pay to obtain it.*)

3.  Use the diagram below to explain electricity generation. Tell students that primary sources, such as coal, oil, uranium (in a reactor), or natural gas, are used to generate heat and steam. Other primary sources, such as wind and water, turn the turbine directly. Explain how the turbine turns the electromagnet in the generator to produce electricity, which is a secondary energy source.

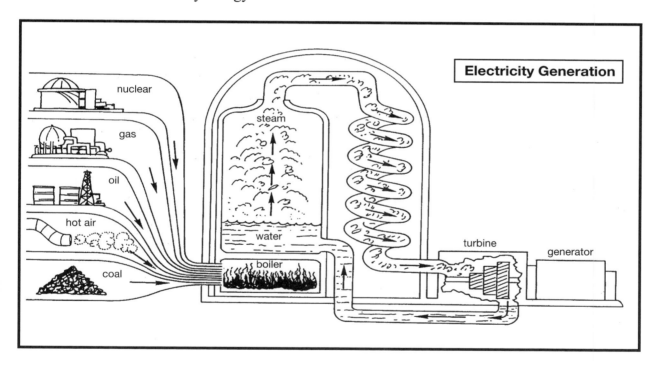

4.  Let students use motions to represent various steps in electrical generation. Steps could include mining, refining, transporting, generation, transmission, etc. Put signs on students identifying what part of the process each student represents.

5.  Have students explore this excellent website about electrical energy: The Electric Universe (www.electricuniverse.com).

6. Have students learn about all kinds of energy sources at this great site: Energy Kid's Page - http://www.eia.doe.gov/kids/energyfacts/index.html

7. For great electrical energy information, go to Electricity InfoCard2004 at http://www.eia.doe.gov/neic/brochure/elecinfocard.html

<u>Map Activity</u>

1. Pass out the U.S. maps and Energy Sources Information Sheet. Identify each state. Students then color code the map to show what type or primary energy is used *most* to generate electricity in that state.

2. After the students have completed the map, discuss why certain types of energy are used in certain states and regions. What source is used most? *(coal)* What factors, besides the local availability of the energy resource, could influence the type of energy used? *(market price of different energy sources, government regulations, transportation costs, political factors)* If a state did not have enough electricity generated locally, what could it do? *(import electricity from another state, region, or country)*

## Teaching Tips:

1. Use a pinwheel to illustrate how a turbine works.

2. For younger students, use maps which have state names.

## Key Questions To Ask Students:

1. "All producers and consumers use energy." True or False? *(True! Have students give examples.)*

2. Why is energy considered a scarce resource? *(It is not freely available in unlimited quantities. It takes scarce productive resources to produce it. One must pay to obtain it.)*

3. What is the difference between a primary and secondary energy source? *(Primary sources are direct renewable or nonrenewable sources that are used to produce secondary sources, such as electricity.)*

4. Why does a state use a particular primary energy source to generate electricity? *(States typically use primary sources that cost less because they are available locally.)*

## Bulletin Board Ideas:

1. Recreate the electricity generation diagram. Put the names of the different primary energy sources on index cards and place them where the energy is used in the generation cycle. (Example: put a "wind" index card near the turbine, an "oil" card near the heat source, etc.) Have students write descriptive paragraphs explaining how electricity is generated. Put these on the bulletin board.

**Student Journal Ideas:**

1. Explain the difference between primary and secondary energy sources.

2. Draw a picture showing how electricity is generated. Write a paragraph explaining the picture.

3. Write a paragraph explaining why you agree or disagree with this statement: "There is a lot of energy. Energy is *not* a scarce resource."

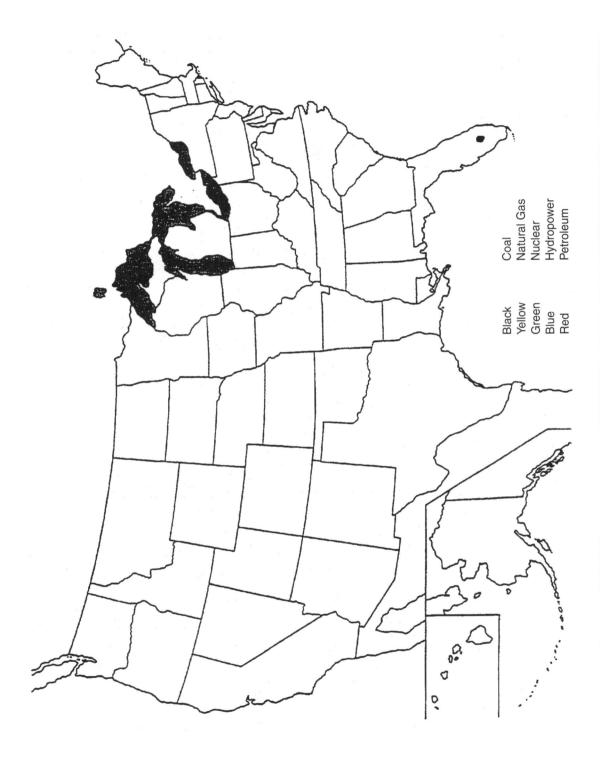

Coal
Natural Gas
Nuclear
Hydropower
Petroleum

Black
Yellow
Green
Blue
Red

# Energy Sources Information Sheet

**Primary Energy Sources Used *Most* to Generate Electricity by State:**

| State | Source | State | Source |
|-------|--------|-------|--------|
| **Alabama** | Coal | **New Hampshire** | Nuclear |
| **Alaska** | Natural Gas | **New Jersey** | Nuclear |
| **Arizona** | Coal | **New Mexico** | Coal |
| **Arkansas** | Coal | **New York** | Nuclear |
| **California** | Natural Gas | **North Carolina** | Coal |
| **Colorado** | Coal | **North Dakota** | Coal |
| **Connecticut** | Nuclear | **Ohio** | Coal |
| **Delaware** | Coal | **Oklahoma** | Coal |
| **District of Columbia** | Petroleum | **Oregon** | Hydroelectric |
| **Florida** | Coal | **Pennsylvania** | Coal |
| **Georgia** | Coal | **Rhode Island** | Natural Gas |
| **Hawaii** | Petroleum | **South Carolina** | Nuclear |
| **Idaho** | Hydroelectric | **South Dakota** | Hydroelectric |
| **Illinois** | Nuclear | **Tennessee** | Coal |
| **Indiana** | Coal | **Texas** | Natural Gas |
| **Iowa** | Coal | **Utah** | Coal |
| **Kansas** | Coal | **Vermont** | Nuclear |
| **Kentucky** | Coal | **Virginia** | Coal |
| **Louisiana** | Natural Gas | **Washington** | Hydroelectric |
| **Maine** | Natural Gas | **West Virginia** | Coal |
| **Maryland** | Coal | **Wisconsin** | Coal |
| **Massachusetts** | Natural Gas | **Wyoming** | Coal |
| **Michigan** | Coal | | |
| **Minnesota** | Coal | | |
| **Mississippi** | Coal | | |
| **Montana** | Coal | | |
| **Nebraska** | Coal | | |
| **Nevada** | Coal | | |

Source: State Electricity Profiles, 2002, Energy Information Administration.

www.eia.doe.gov

# Electricity

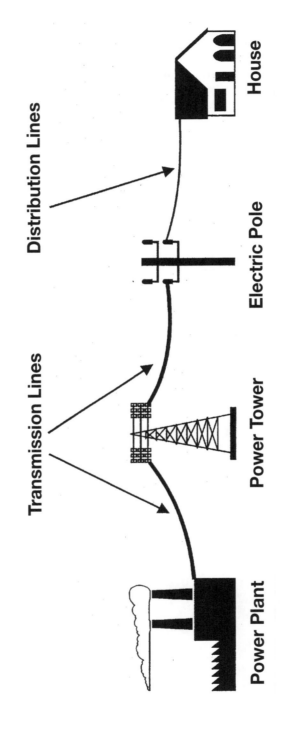

Transmission Lines

Distribution Lines

Power Plant

Power Tower

Electric Pole

House

**Electricity is the flow of electrons through wires.**

# Activity 3
## Energy Search

**Teaching Objectives:** After completing this activity, students will:

1. Identify and define the three basic productive resources.
2. Explain that the search for energy sources will necessarily impact the environment.
3. Explain why the marginal cost of finding and extracting energy resources eventually increases.
4. Predict that as the cost of fossil fuels increases, other energy sources will be used.
5. Explain why we will never "run out" of nonrenewable energy resources.

**Time Allowed:**   30 minutes

**Materials:**
- Four colors of beads (100 black, 6 red, 20 white, 74 blue)
- Several tablespoons of cornmeal
- 1/4 cup of oatmeal

## Vocabulary:

- *Scarcity:* the condition of not being able to have all of the goods, services, or productive resources that you want. Energy is considered *scarce* because it is not freely available in unlimited quantities.

- *Price:* the amount people pay to buy a good, service, or productive resource. Prices reflect *relative scarcity.* Items which are more scarce generally cost more than those which are not.

- *Productive Resources:* the inputs (natural, human, and capital) needed to produce goods and services

Energy is used in all production and consumption. Energy resources are **scarce natural resources** and must be extracted from nature to be used. Locating and extracting energy resources will always impact the environment to some degree. Repairing environmental damage increases the cost of producing energy.

There are still vast quantities of nonrenewable energy resources in the earth's crust. However, as companies search for and extract energy resources it typically becomes more costly, since the resources are more difficult to find, are located in more inaccessible places, etc. If a nonrenewable resource becomes relatively more **scarce,** its **market price** will rise, causing consumers to use less. The high price makes the use of alternative energy resources more attractive and encourages their development. This is why we will never "run out" of energy.

## Teaching Procedure:

1. While students are out of the room, randomly scatter the beads, cornmeal, and oatmeal. Hide some of the beads and cornmeal under items to make them more difficult to find.

2. Divide the class into six energy companies. Each company will search for a specific material (color of bead, oatmeal, or cornmeal). Explain that you have thrown an unknown quantity of energy resources in the classroom. Students must recover as much as possible within a given period of time. Let the companies meet to discuss "mining" strategies.

3. Have companies conduct a one-minute energy search. Then reassemble the companies. Have them count their beads or measure the amount of oatmeal or cornmeal. Record the totals for each company on the blackboard or overhead.

4. Start a second one-minute search for any resources not yet found. Each company must make a new pile of any newly found resources. Reassemble and record totals.

5. Start a third one-minute search and record results.

6. Discuss questions in the Key Questions To Ask Students section below.

## Teaching Tips:

1. If you increase the number of beads, keep them in the same proportions.

2. The beads can represent specific energy sources: black – coal; white – natural gas; red – uranium; blue – petroleum; cornmeal – solar; oatmeal – hydropower. The cornmeal is diffused and hard to gather. This represents the high cost (in terms of productive resources) of producing solar energy. Until these costs decrease, solar will not be as widely used as other sources.

3. If any company gathers some other colors, do not interfere or comment.

4. Adjust the amount of search time if students locate the beads too quickly.

## Key Questions To Ask Students:

1. What productive resources were used in your energy search? *(Mainly labor was used. In real life, it also takes a lot of capital, such as drilling equipment, etc.)*

2. What do you notice about the piles of beads? *(They are smaller in each round.)*

3. Which search cost your company more? Why? *(The second and third. The beads were harder to find. In the same amount of time, we gathered less. People may not have looked as hard.)*

4. What made the beads easier or more difficult to find? Was it the availability of the beads or the skill of the searchers? *(Both are important.)*

5. Did it help your company to discuss how to mine before the first search? Explain. *(It probably helped. Companies could plan their search strategies.)*

6. How could a company have gathered more beads in a specific time period? *(Use a broom or vacuum cleaner – capital equipment.)*

7. As energy becomes more scarce and demand for energy increases, what should happen to its price? *(The price should rise.)*

8. Did you change your "environment" as you searched? How? *(Yes. We moved books, furniture, etc. Relate this movement to strip mining and other environmental impacts.)*

9. If you moved things to uncover your beads, did you move them back? *(Yes. Relate this to the costs of repairing land damaged by strip mining, energy extraction, etc.)* What was the "opportunity cost" of doing so? *(The oportunity cost was the time lost looking for more beads. In real life, it takes many costly productive resources to restore land that has been mined.)*

10. What would happen if the teacher paid you 25 cents for every bead found? What about 50 cents? As the price increases what incentives do you have? *(You have an incentive to find more beads! At higher prices, energy producers will expend more productive resources to find energy.)*

## Bulletin Board Ideas:

1. "Environmental Effects of Using Energy Sources." List the different energy resources across the board. Divide the students into cooperative groups and assign a resource to each group. After discussing the effects on the environment of using this resource, have groups of students write the effects on index cards and place them below the resource name. Find or draw pictures which illustrate these ideas.

## Student Journal Ideas:

1. Write a paragraph entitled, "What I Learned in the Energy Search Activity."

2. Explain why you think it is important to "fix" the environment after energy exploration has occurred.

3. If we did this activity again and you were in charge of mining, what would be your directions to your search team?

4. Describe the different types of jobs involved in energy production.

---

(This activity was adapted from *Energy Tradeoffs in the Marketplace*, published by the Washington State Superintendent of Public Instruction Office and the Washington State Council on Economic Education, [Seattle, WA; 1980] pp. 51-55.)

# Activity 4
## Energy Efficiency

**Teaching Objectives:**  After completing this activity, students will be able to:

1. Define and explain energy efficiency.
2. Identify specific ways to improve energy efficiency.
3. Explain why increasing energy efficiency sometimes conflicts with other economic goals.
4. Explain the role of market price in energy conservation.

**Time Allowed:**   Two 30-minute sessions

**Materials:**
- Chart paper/bulletin board
- Examples of items to be recycled or reused.  (Paper sacks,  aluminum cans, etc., brought by students.)
- Conservation Plan worksheet
- Decision Tree of Five-Step Model worksheets (pages 19-20)
- Choice Cards

**Vocabulary/Concepts:**

- *Economic Efficiency:*  getting the most benefit from *all* of our scarce productive resources

- *Energy Efficiency:*  getting the maximum use/greatest benefit from scarce energy resources

- *Price:*  the amount people pay to buy a good, service, or productive resource.  Prices reflect *relative scarcity.*

- *Reduce:*  to lower consumption

- *Reuse:*  to use a product again for the same or another purpose

- *Recycle:*  putting waste through a cycle of purification and conversion to make a useful product

Increasing **energy efficiency** means getting more work done with the same amount of energy.  This results in better **energy conservation**.  Sometimes increasing energy efficiency conflicts with other economic goals.  For example, the United States could make automobiles today that average 100 miles per gallon.  This would promote energy efficiency/conservation, but the autos would have less power, crash protection, and payload capability.  Actually, the best way to conserve energy would be to use no energy at all!  This, of course, is not feasible and would be very detrimental to overall **economic efficiency**.  The **market price** guides consumers and producers in their energy decisions.  Energy resources that have higher prices are relatively more **scarce** than those with lower prices.  A high price for an energy resource encourages consumers to use less and energy producers to provide more.

## Teaching Procedure:

1. Write the words, "Energy Conservation" on the blackboard or overhead. Brainstorm ideas generated by this term and create a concept map/word web.

2. Introduce the term **energy efficiency** (*getting the best use/maximum benefit from scarce energy resources*). Explain that increasing energy efficiency is a good way to conserve energy resources. Discuss ways of increasing energy efficiency around the home. (*adding insulation, engines with better fuel economy, appliances that use less electricity, fuel efficient furnaces, etc.*)

3. On the board, write the three words: **reuse, reduce, recycle**. Discuss their meanings, and list their definitions on the board. Explain that these words are often used to explain ways consumers and producers can conserve natural resources, including energy resources.

4. Take three colors of chalk and color code the words **reuse, reduce,** and **recycle**. Go back to the original list of generated ideas on energy conservation and have students identify into which category (reuse, reduce, or recycle) each idea falls. (*Most will probably concern reducing the amount of energy needed to do a certain task.*) Circle with the appropriate color chalk.

5. Ask students if producers and consumers should always improve their energy efficiency. (*Most will agree, but the answer is not always clear cut!*) Read and discuss the following scenario:

---

Mrs. Smith is a very busy person. She is a teacher, is married, and has two children. She also helps with the Girl Scouts, teaches Sunday School, and coaches a girls' softball team. To clean her house, she uses an electric vacuum cleaner. Should she uses a broom instead of a vacuum cleaner? She would save energy (be more energy efficient) if she did.

---

(*Point out that using a broom would be more **energy efficient**, but it probably would not be the best choice. i.e., would not be **economically efficient**. Mrs. Smith must consider how to use all her productive resources – including her limited time. Using a vacuum cleaner and other handy appliances frees up time to do other valuable things. A vacuum cleaner also does a better job, especially on carpets, than a broom.*)

6. Discuss the importance of **price** in energy conservation. Emphasize that as the real price of an energy resource rises (indicating that it is becoming relatively more scarce), consumers and producers react in predictable ways. Consumers use less and producers supply more. At lower prices, the reverse is true.

7. **<u>Group Work:  Energy Choices Cards</u>**

      **Task 1:**  Divide students into groups of four or five.  Give each group a Choice Card and use the Decision Tree or Five-Step Model to decide what to do.  Make sure students list various good and bad points about each choice and the energy **trade-offs** that are involved.  Have each group explain its decision to the class.  Discuss group choices.

      **Task 2:**  Tell groups to create new scenarios for new Choice Cards.  Exchange these new Choice Cards and use the Decision Tree or Five-Step Model.

      **Task 3:**  Develop an Energy Conservation Plan that identifies ways to make homes energy efficient.

## Teaching Tips:

1.      Explaining the difference between **energy efficiency** and **economic efficiency** is challenging.  Giving extreme examples, such as not taking showers to save electricity or banning automobiles to save oil, helps clarify these concepts.  Remember, the goal is to maximize the efficiency of *all* of our productive resources (human and capital, as well as natural), not just to maximize energy efficiency.

## Key Questions To Ask Students:

1.      What is "energy efficiency?"  *(getting the most benefit from energy resources)*

2.      What are ways to increase energy efficiency in your home?  *(adding insulation, buying more energy efficient appliances, walking to work, etc.)*

3.      Should people always maximize their energy efficiency?  *(Not necessarily - being a good steward means maximizing the efficiency of <u>all</u> productive resources.  This may mean using a machine, which uses energy, to save valuable time.)*

4.      How does a higher price for energy help conserve energy?  *(At higher prices, consumers and producers will use less energy.)*

5.      How does a higher price for energy help make energy more available?  *(A higher price that results in more profits encourages energy producers to search for and develop more energy resources.)*

## Bulletin Board Ideas:

1.      Make a "Ways to Save Energy" bulletin board.

2.      Display the Decision Tree solutions and Conservation Plans.

## Student Journal Ideas:

1.      Write and illustrate a poem about saving energy in your home.
2.      Write and illustrate a paragraph entitled, "How to Make a Home Energy Efficient."
3.      Create a play about Mr. Jones, a homeowner who wants to insulate his home.  Include some of the tough decisions he must think through.

# Energy Choice Cards

**Scenario 1:** John has a lawn mower service. He wants to make as much money as possible to save for college. On small lawns, he could use his old push mower, which still works but takes much longer. Using his power mower would help him earn more money, but would use gasoline and cause more pollution. What should he do?

**Scenario 2:** Ms. Johnson works in an insurance office. She lives two miles away and drives a Ford Focus to work each day. She could ride a bicycle to work, but this would mean leaving earlier each day and could be a problem in very cold weather. Also, she doesn't feel safe walking. Walking would save energy, however. Should she walk or continue to use her car?

**Scenario 3:** Mr. Williams drives a lot on his job as a sales person. He owns a large, comfortable SUV that gets about 22 mpg on the highway. He is considering saving energy by buying a much smaller car that gets 40 mpg. However, he is concerned that the smaller car is not as comfortable or safe, and it would not provide as much space for his wife and three children, especially on vacations. Should he buy the smaller car?

**Scenario 4:** Mr. and Mrs. Crawford want to reduce their electric bills. They currently pay $50 each month, but figure that they can reduce that to $45 by insulating their house. It will cost $500 to insulate the house. Should they do it? (Hint: Does the price of the insulation influence your decision?)

**Scenario 5:** The students in Centerville Elementary believe in recycling. They recycle almost all of the classroom paper that used to be thrown away. Some of the students now want to recycle the paper napkins that are thrown away in the school cafeteria. Should this be done?

**Scenario 6:** There is a long hedge around Mr. Jones' house. To keep the hedge from getting too tall, he trims it every month using hand-held clippers. His wife suggests that buying an electric hedge trimmer would save him a lot of time, even though this would mean using a bit more electricity each month. Should Mr. Jones buy the electric trimmer?

**Scenario 7:** Mrs. Johnson is a very busy person. She works part-time at a flower shop, volunteers at the public library, and is involved in many of her two children's activities. She lives on the bus line, but doesn't take the bus much any more, even though the bus could take her to many of the activities. She wants to have the freedom to come and go quickly without waiting for the bus, especially in bad weather! Taking the bus would save energy. Should she quit using her car and use the bus instead?

**Scenario 8:** Mr. Calloway is 78 years old and not in good health. When he was younger, he kept his thermostat at 68 degrees in the winter. Because of his age and health, he now keeps his house very warm at about 74 degrees. This takes a lot more energy. Should he lower his thermostat back to 68 degrees?

# Conservation Plan

**Name** _____

Below are things we can do to improve energy efficiency at home.

1.

2.

3.

4.

5.

6.

**Answer these questions about your Conservation Plan:**

What **trade-offs** are involved in your plan?

What will you have to give up? (What are your **opportunity costs?**)

How will your family's lifestyle change as a result of your plan? How do members of your family feel about the changes in lifestyle?

# Activity 5
## Further Explorations

1. Survey ten people in your community to find out:
   a. Do you carpool, walk, or ride a bicycle to work or school?
   b. Do you use any kind of public transportation to get to work or school?
   c. Would you be willing to use these types of transportation? Why or why not?

2. Research the history of solar energy. How did ancient people use this form of energy? What developments have taken place in the past 100 years? Why isn't it used more today?

3. Research the term "mass transit system." Where are these systems currently being used? What are the advantages and disadvantages?

4. Prepare a report on how electricity is generated on wind farms. Describe and draw the different types of wind generators. What are the advantages and disadvantages of these farms? In which states are most wind farms located?

5. Explain how a hydroelectric power plant operates. Label your diagram. List the benefits of hydropower. Identify some of the environmental concerns about constructing this type of power plant.

6. Research the location of coal deposits in the United States. What economic impact does coal mining have in different regions of the country? What are the different types of coal? How are they different? Where are they located?

7. Research the advantages and disadvantages of using wood as a fuel. Investigate how wood was used in the past and how it is used today. Research some of the new trends in wood use, including the new "super trees."

8. Research which countries of the world rely on nuclear energy. Why do they do so? What do they do with the radioactive waste? How efficient is electricity produced using nuclear power? Have there been any safety problems with this type of energy?

9. Investigate the cost of electricity in your community. How does it compare with the cost in other communities, states, and regions of the United States? How is electricity use measured?

10. Research natural gas supplies in your community. How is it transported? Where are natural gas resources located? How is natural gas use measured? What is the cost of natural gas? How does the cost compare with other energy sources?

# Activity 6
## Let's Talk It Over

Energy efficiency in the United States has improved greatly during the past 34 years. For example, from 1970 to 2004, per capita energy consumption rose slightly from 334 million BTUs to 340 BTUs. However, consumption per dollar of Gross Domestic Product (GDP) declined from 17.99 to 9.2 thousand BTUs. In other words, in 2004 it took only about one half the amount of energy to produce a dollar of GDP than in 1970!

However, because the United States is such a large country and consumes a large amount of energy, some individuals believe that the United States is not doing enough to increase its energy efficiency. Below are some controversial statements for your students to discuss/debate. Help students think critically by applying the concepts learned in this unit.

<u>To increase energy efficiency and help conserve our energy resources:</u>

1.    Schools should close during December and January and open in June and July, with no air conditioning allowed.

2.    Everyone should be required to keep thermostats at 68 degrees.

3.    All students must take the school bus if they don't walk or ride bicycles.

4.    Families should not be allowed to own more than two vehicles.

5.    The tax on gasoline should be raised significantly.

6.    Large SUV and van owners should pay an extra "large vehicle tax."

7.    The driving age should be raised to 21 so that fewer people would be driving cars.

8.    Car companies should be required to produce solar-powered cars.

9.    People should be required to purchase solar-powered cars, even if they cost more, have less power, have less passenger and storage space, and are not as safe because of their smaller size.

10.    Electric companies should be required to generate some of their electricity using wind or solar power, even if this means higher electric bills for customers.

11.    We should let the market price of energy guide the energy decisions of producers and consumers. We should not restrict the freedom of choice in energy matters.

# Activity 7
## EEE Actions:  You Can Make a Difference!

Below are suggestions for conserving energy and other natural resources:

1.   Write on both sides of the paper that you use.  Use scrap paper for notes and lists.

2.   If feasible, walk or ride a bicycle or bus to activities.

3.   Plant shade trees around your house.  This will make your home cooler and reduce the need for air conditioning

4.   Dress for the season.  In the winter, wear warm clothing inside your house and turn down the thermostat.  In the summer, wear cool, loose clothes.  These steps will let you turn your thermostat down some and use your air conditioning less.

5.   Reuse, reduce, and recycle where feasible (especially aluminum, which requires a lot of energy to produce).

6.   Make sure that the family car has a regular tune-up.  Keep the tires properly inflated.

7.   Conduct an energy audit for your school.  Suggest ways to make your school more energy-efficient.  Discuss your audit with the principal.  Present your findings to the student council.

8.   Create energy conservation posters and put them in the school hallways and other public buildings.

9.   Publish a school newsletter describing ways that everyone can conserve at home and at school.

10.  During cold weather, lower your thermostat at night.

11.  Use light bulbs that require less electricity.

12.  Use appliances efficiently.  For example, run dishwashers and washing machines with full loads.  Wash clothes in cold water, don't overheat your hot water, use a clothes line instead of the dryer in warm weather, and buy energy-efficient appliances.

13.  Don't take long showers.  It takes energy to heat water.

14.  Insulate your home more effectively, especially doors and windows.

# Activity 8
## The Case of the Outdoor Lab

**Student Directions:** In this case study, you will help some students solve a problem. Divide into groups of five, read the scenario, and then use the Decision Tree or Five-Step Model worksheet to make a decision. Then carefully answer the questions below.

---

### Scenario

The teachers and students of Yellow River Elementary have an interesting problem. The students have developed a large outdoor laboratory on eight acres of land next to the school. There is a variety of trees and wildlife on the property. They are also planning to construct a large pond to develop water habitats for animals.

Last week, a geologist from a small oil company conducted an energy survey and discovered a large oil deposit in the middle of the eight acres. "If five or six oil wells were put into operation," said the geologist, "the school is guaranteed $200,000 a year for five years, and maybe more after that." Unfortunately, developing the oil wells would mean giving up the outdoor laboratory.

The whole community is divided over the issue. Those who favor the oil wells argue that the additional money could help build a new gym, increase teacher salaries, or buy new equipment for the school. Using oil produced in the United States would also reduce our dependence on oil imports.

Those who oppose the oil wells don't want to give up the school's new outdoor lab, especially since there is no other land available near the school. Opponents also think the oil wells are ugly and would harm wildlife habitats.

The school board is considering the proposal. Your group has been asked to serve on a committee to look into all the possible effects and to make a recommendation.

---

1.	What is your group's recommendation/decision? _____

_____

_____

2.  How would this decision affect the community? _____

_____

_____

_____

_____

3.  What is the **opportunity cost** of your group's decision? _____

_____

_____

_____

4.  What are the **trade-offs** that are involved in this decision? _____

_____

_____

_____

_____

# Answers to Selected Teaching Activities

## Activity 8: Decision Tree Model

*Develop Oil Wells:* <u>Good Points</u>: Gains much income for the school for various purposes, helps reduce our dependence on oil imports. <u>Bad Points</u>: School loses adjacent outdoor lab, some damage to wildlife habitat and environment, unsightly.

*Develop Outdoor Lab:* <u>Good Points</u>: Students could learn about ecology, etc., good habitat for animals, attractive setting around school. <u>Bad Points</u>: Lose significant amount of money by not developing oil wells, keeps the United States more dependent on oil imports.

## Five Step Model:

| **Decision-Making Grid Answer Key** <br> **The Case of the Outdoor Lab** | | | | |
|---|---|---|---|---|
| **Criteria** | | | | |
| **Alternatives** | **Tax Revenues/Money** | **Wildlife Habitat** | **Scenic Beauty** | **Dependence on Oil Imports** |
| **Develop Oil Resources** | + | - | - | + |
| **Keep Outdoor Lab** | - | + | + | - |

1. Answers will vary.

2. Developing the oil wells would bring much needed money to the school corporation, keeping down taxes. There probably would be more business activity in the community. Keeping the outdoor lab would not have as much direct impact. The community would not have increased business activity (and the associated tax revenues), but would have more of an environmental focus.

3. The decision <u>not</u> chosen.

4. The main trade-offs are economic growth versus the environmental quality. Other trade-offs associated with these involve the beauty of the landscape, wildlife habitat concerns, jobs, and the amount of tax revenues gained or lost.

# EEE Resources

## General Resources

United States Environmental Protection Agency - www.epa.gov

Indiana Department of Education – www.doe.state.in.us

Indiana Council for Economic Education - www.econed-in.org

Indiana Department of Environmental Management – www.in.gov/idem

Indiana Department of Natural Resources - www.state.in.us/dnr

National Geographic Society - www.nationalgeographic.com

## Water Quality Resources

Union of Concerned Scientists   www.ucsusa.org

American Groundwater Trust - www.agwt.org

American Water Works Association - www.awwa.org

Federal Drinking Water Hotline – www.epa.gov/safewater/hotline/index.html

Izaak Walton League of America – www.iwla.org

Lake Michigan Federation – www.great-lakes.net/lakes/michigan

Alliance for the Great Lakes -  www.lakemichigan.org

United States Geological Survey – www.usgs.gov

Water Environmental Federation – www.wef.org

## Forest Resources

About Forestry – www.forestry.about.com

American Forest Research Council – www.growthevote.org

American Forestry Foundation – www.affoundation.org

American Forest and Paper Association – www.afandpa.org

American Tree Farm System – www.treefarmsystem.org

Indiana Wildlife Federation – www.indianawildlife.org

Indiana Department of Natural Resources, Division of Forestry – www.in.gov/dnr/forestry

National Arbor Day Foundation – www.arborday.org

National Audubon Society – www.audubon.org

National Wildlife Federation – www.nwf.org

Society of American Foresters –  www.safnet.org

The Wilderness Society – www.wilderness.org

United States Department of Agriculture – Forest Services – www.fs.fed.us

United States Fish and Wildlife Service, Department of the Interior – www.fws.gov/index.html

# Energy Resources

The Alliance to Save Energy – www.ase.org

American Council for an Energy Efficient Economy –  www.aceee.org

American Electric Power (AEP) – www.aep.com

American Electric Power (AEP) Teacher Grants –

www.aep.com/about/community/teacherGrants/default.htm

Electric Universe (for kids) – www.electricuniverse.com

American Solar Energy Society –  www.ases.org

American Wind Energy Association – www.awea.org

CINERGY/PSI Energy – www.cinergypsi.com/default.asp

Citizens Gas and Coke Utility –  www.citizensgas.com

Energy Efficiency and Renewable Energy – www.eere.energy.gov

Electricity Information Card - www.eia.doe.gov/neic/brochure/elecinfocard.html

Energy Information Administration – www.eia.doe.gov

Energy Kid's Page - www.eia.doe.gov/kids/energyfacts/index.html

Geothermal Education Office – www.geothermal.marin.org